Shiplake (Stage 10)

THE THAMES PATH

The Thames Path is an official National Trail covering 182 miles from Woolwich Foot Tunnel in London, passing through rural countryside on its course to the river's source in Gloucestershire. This book provides full information and mapping for this easy riverside route that takes around two weeks to complete.

Contents and using this guide

This booklet of Ordnance Survey 1:25,000 Explorer® maps has been designed for convenient use on the trail and includes:
- a key to map pages (pages 2–3) showing where to find the maps for each stage.
- the full and up-to-date line of the National Trail designed for use whether you are walking eastbound or westbound.
- an extract from the OS Explorer map legend (pages 90–92).

In addition, the *Thames Path* guidebook describes the full route from east to west (including the unofficial but increasingly popular section from Erith to the Woolwich Foot Tunnel) with lots of other practical and historical information.

© Cicerone Press 2023
ISBN: 978 1 78631 149 8
Reprinted 2025
Photos © Leigh Hatts 2023
© Crown copyright and database rights 2023 OS AC0000810376
Printed in China on responsibly sourced paper on behalf of Latitude Press Ltd

MIX
Paper | Supporting responsible forestry
FSC® C010256

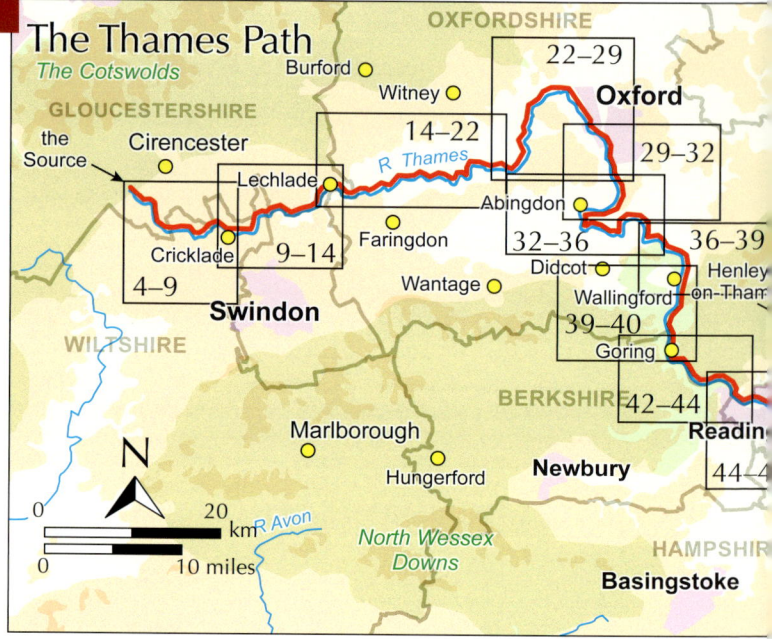

THE THAMES PATH

Stages run east to west, from London to the Source, as described in *The Thames Path* companion guidebook but maps run west to east for ease of comprehension!

Prelude	Woolwich Foot Tunnel to Erith	89
Stage 1	Woolwich Foot Tunnel to Tower Bridge	86
Stage 2	Tower Bridge to Putney	82
Stage 3	Putney to Kingston	78
Stage 4	Kingston to Chertsey	72
Stage 5	Chertsey to Staines	66
Stage 6	Staines to Windsor	65
Stage 7	Windsor to Maidenhead	63
Stage 8	Maidenhead to Marlow	58
Stage 9	Marlow to Henley	55
Stage 10	Henley to Reading	52
Stage 11	Reading to Pangbourne	47
Stage 12	Pangbourne to Goring	44
Stage 13	Goring to Wallingford	40
Stage 14	Wallingford to Dorchester	39

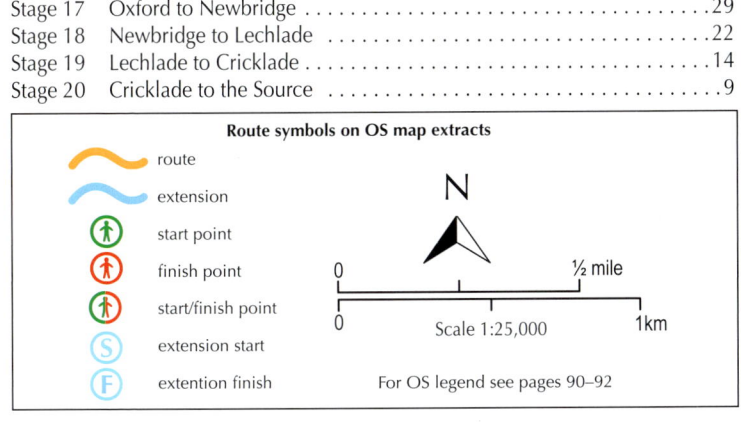

Stage 15	Dorchester to Abingdon	36
Stage 16	Abingdon to Oxford	32
Stage 17	Oxford to Newbridge	29
Stage 18	Newbridge to Lechlade	22
Stage 19	Lechlade to Cricklade	14
Stage 20	Cricklade to the Source	9

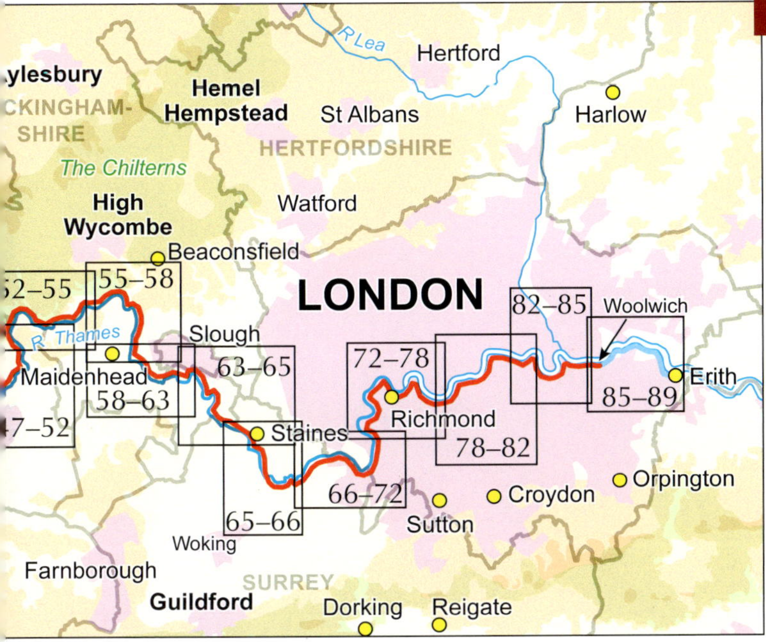

Route symbols on OS map extracts

- route
- extension
- start point
- finish point
- start/finish point
- S extension start
- F extention finish

N

0 — ½ mile
0 — 1km
Scale 1:25,000

For OS legend see pages 90–92

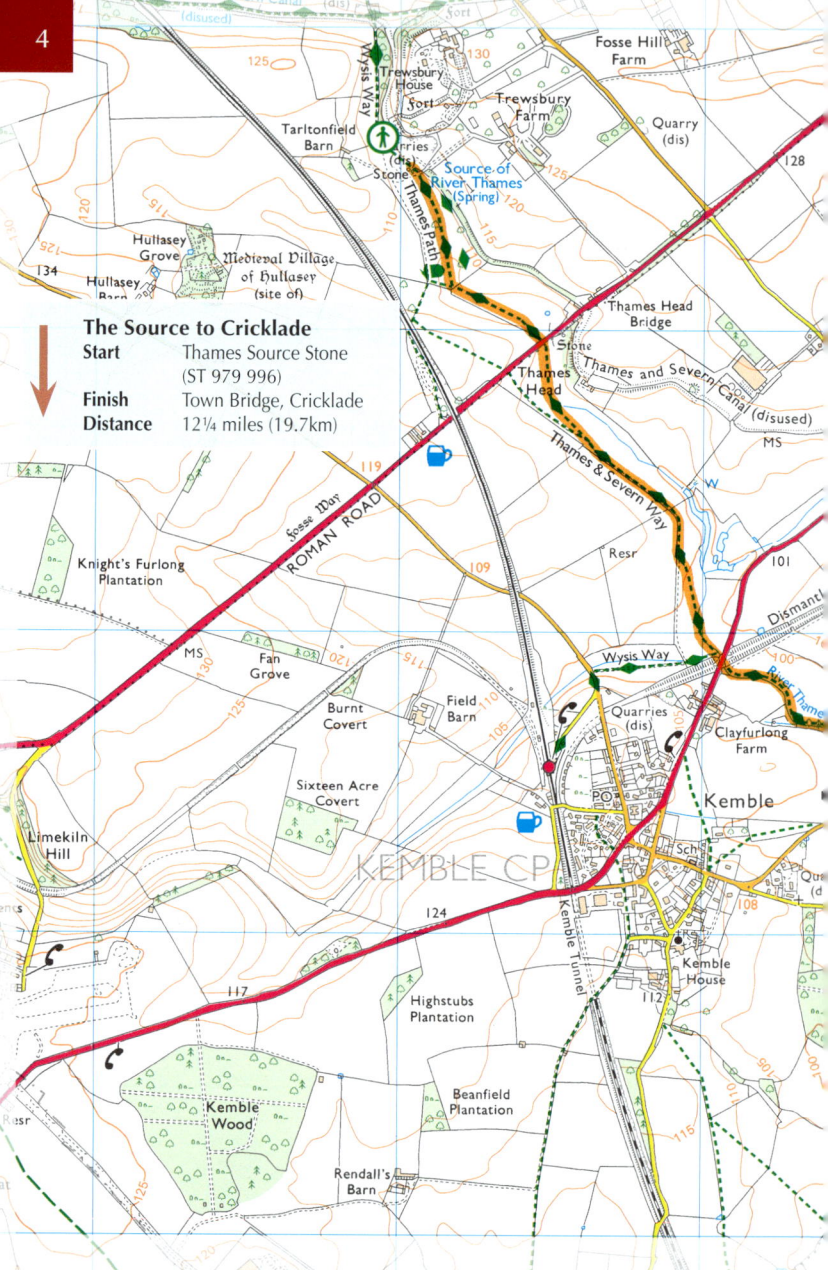

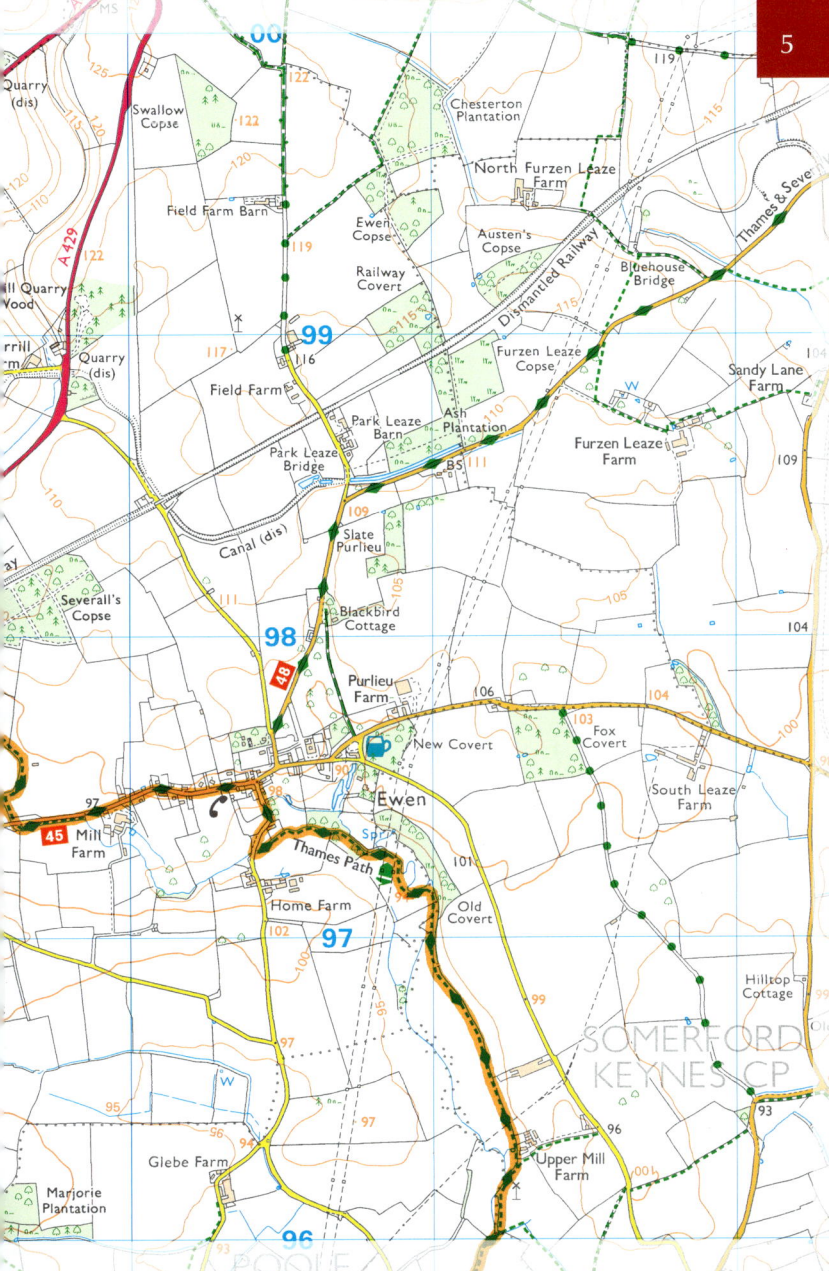

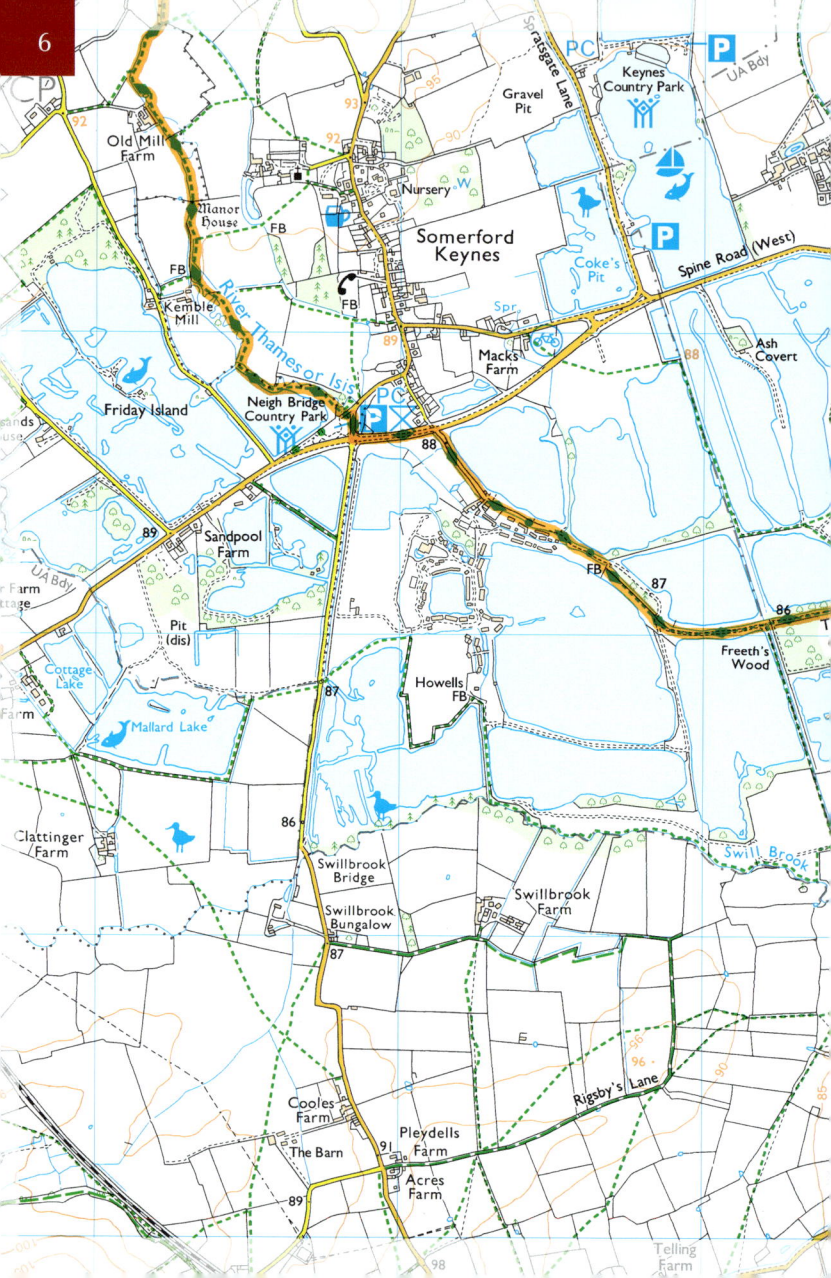

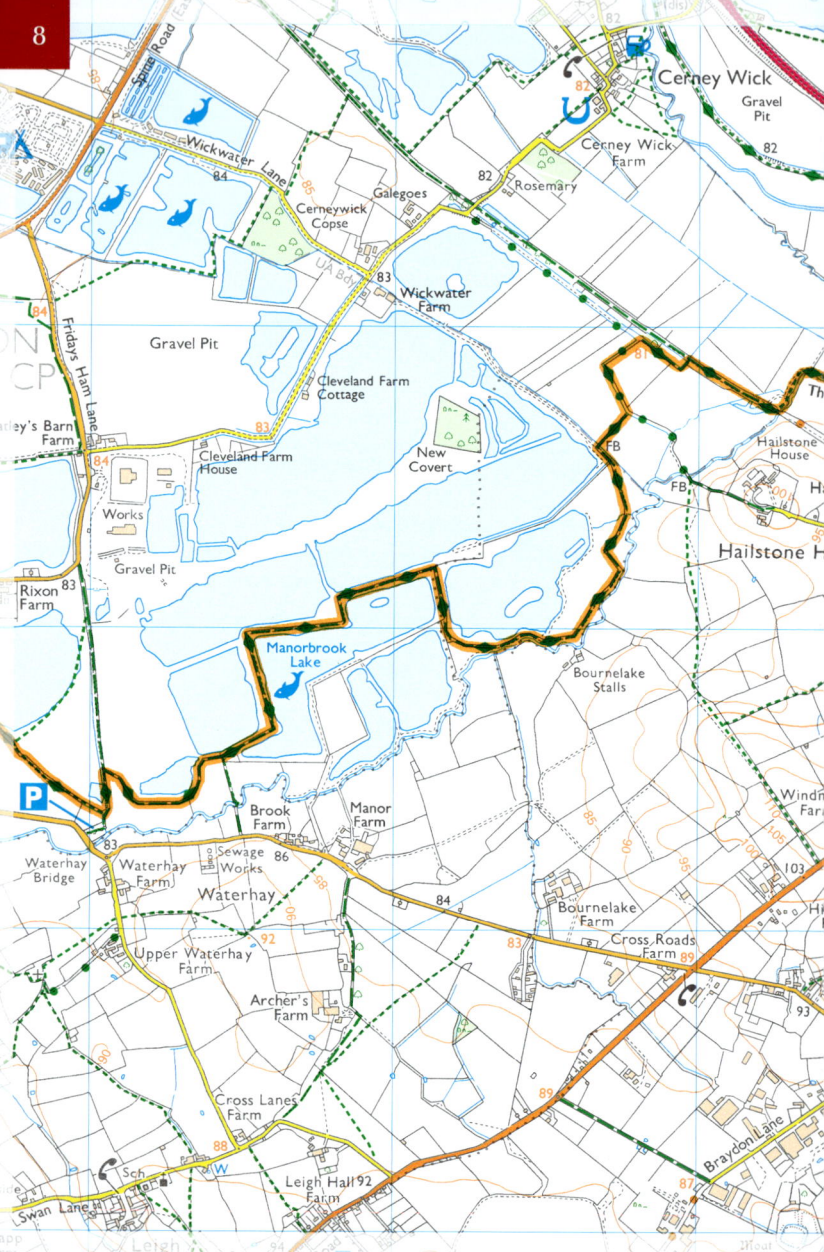

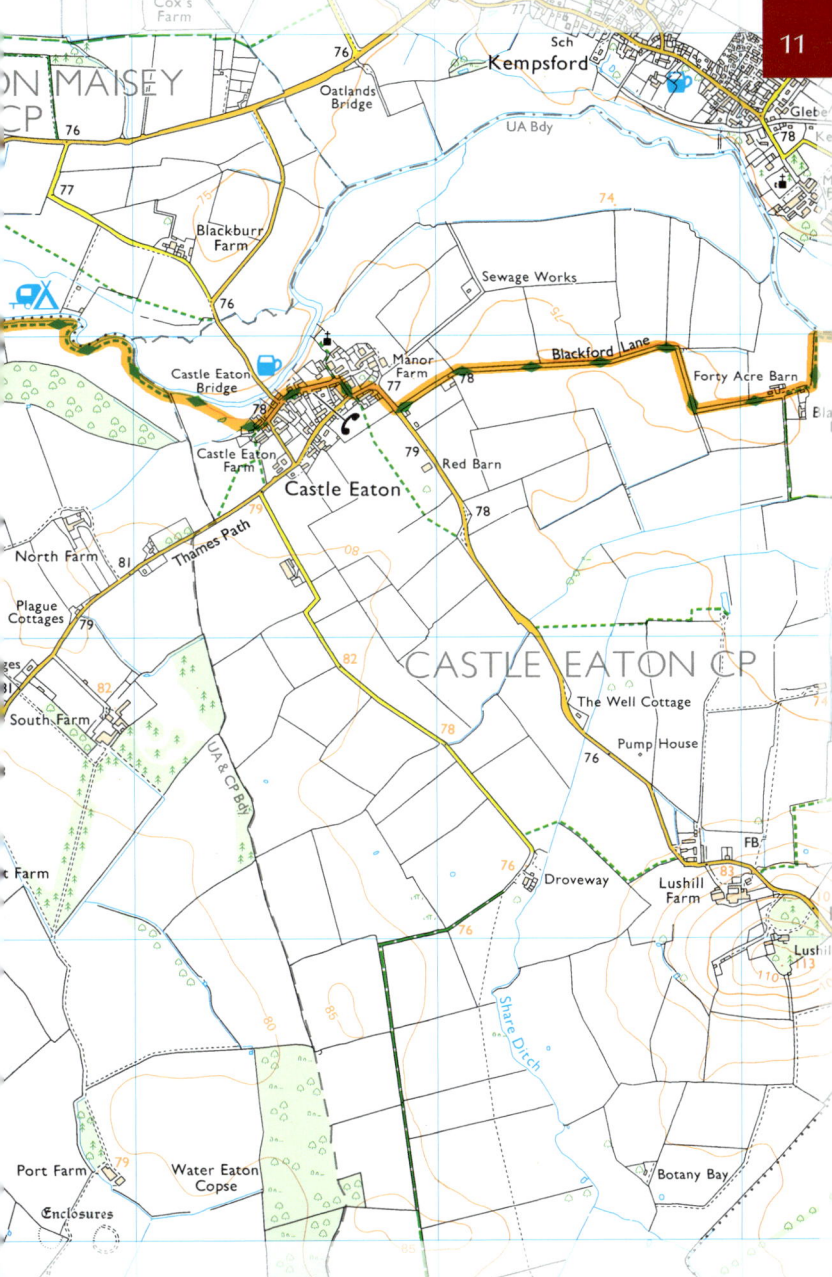

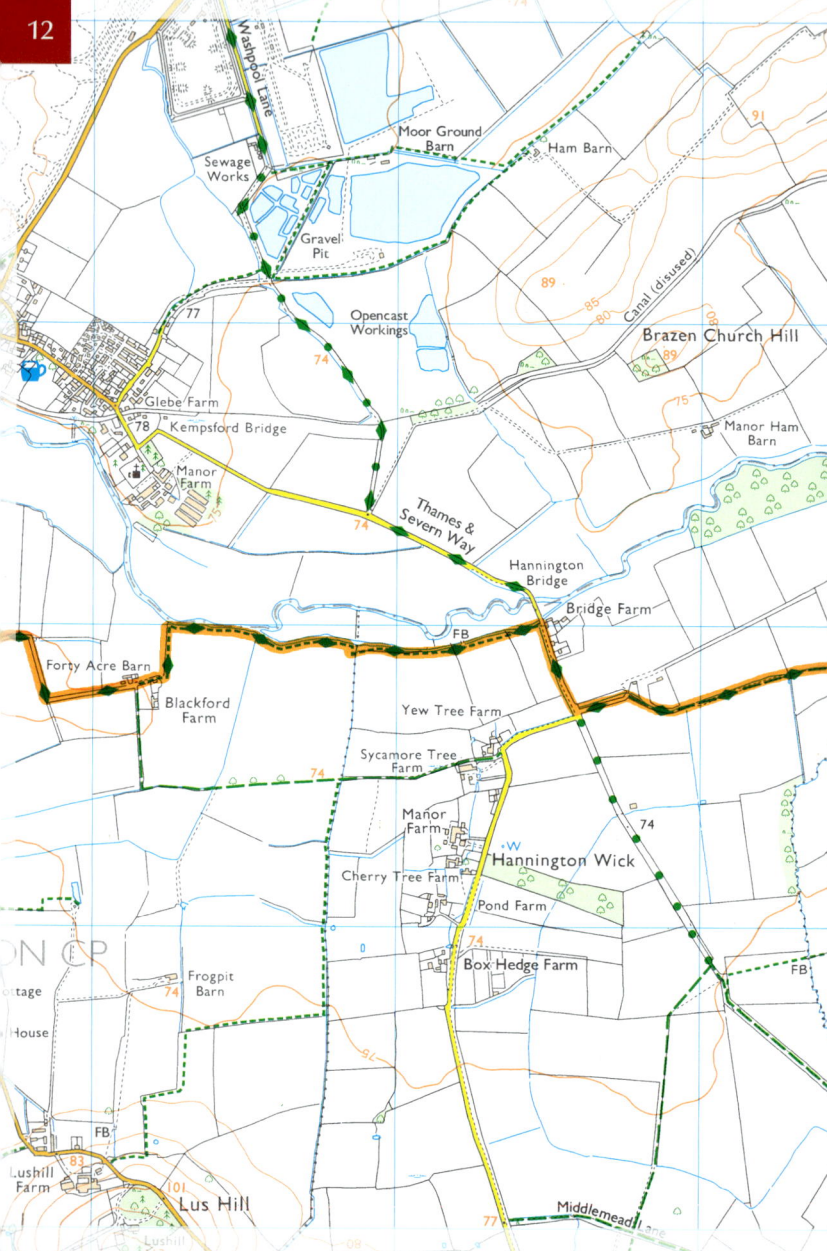

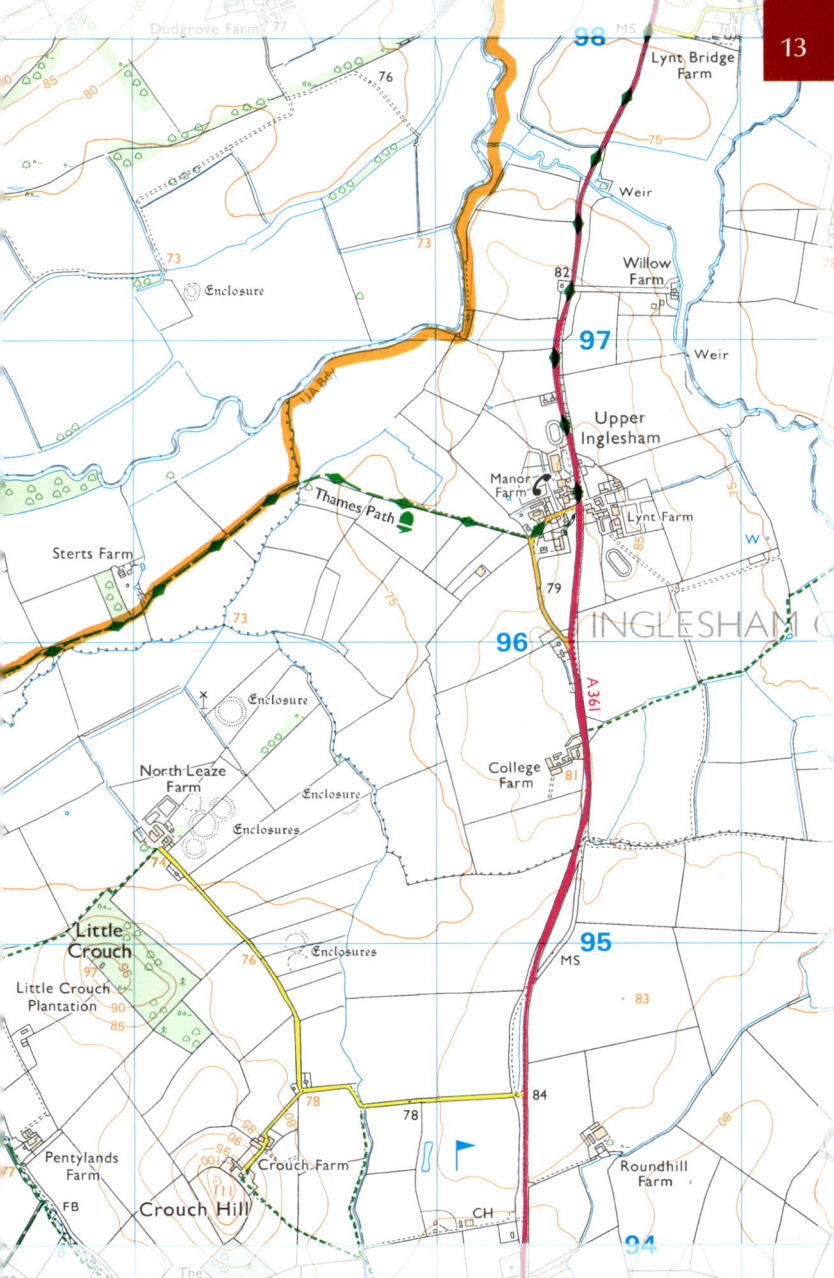

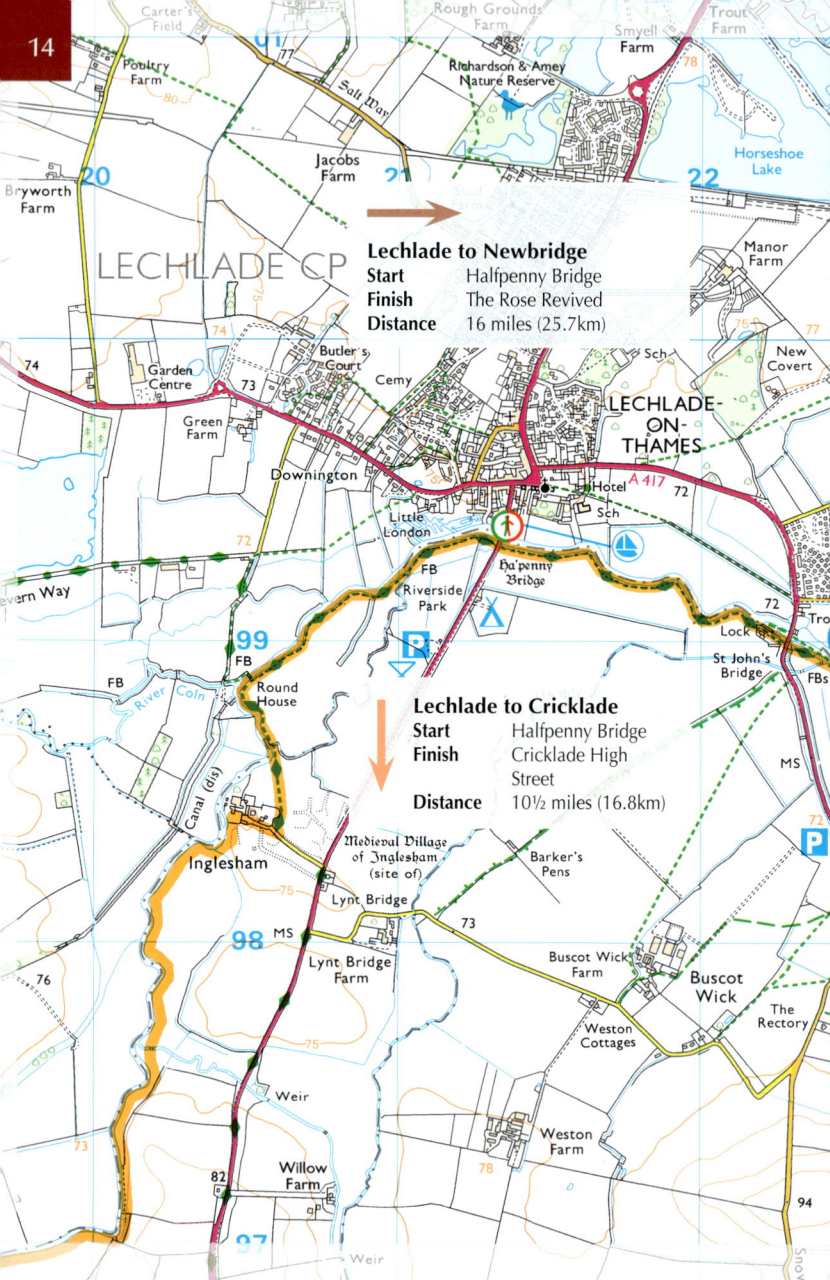

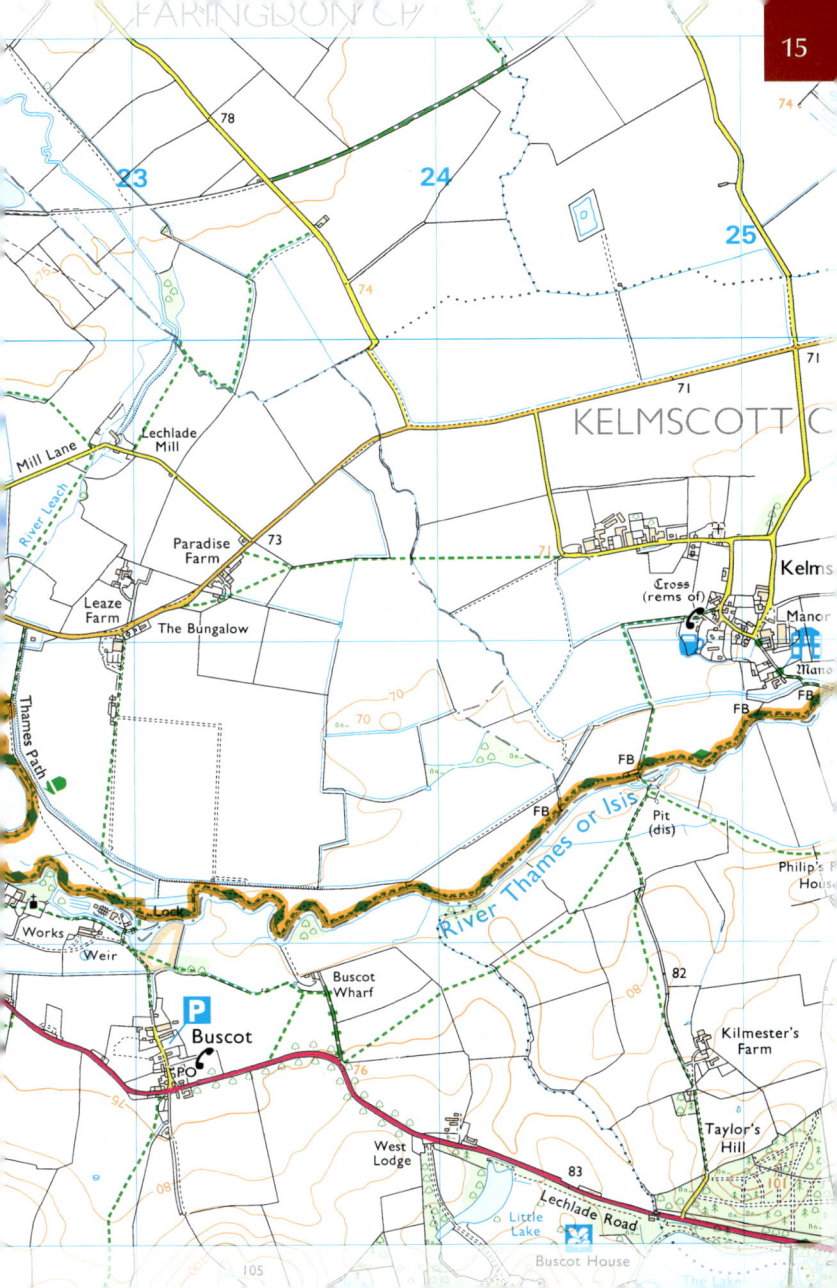

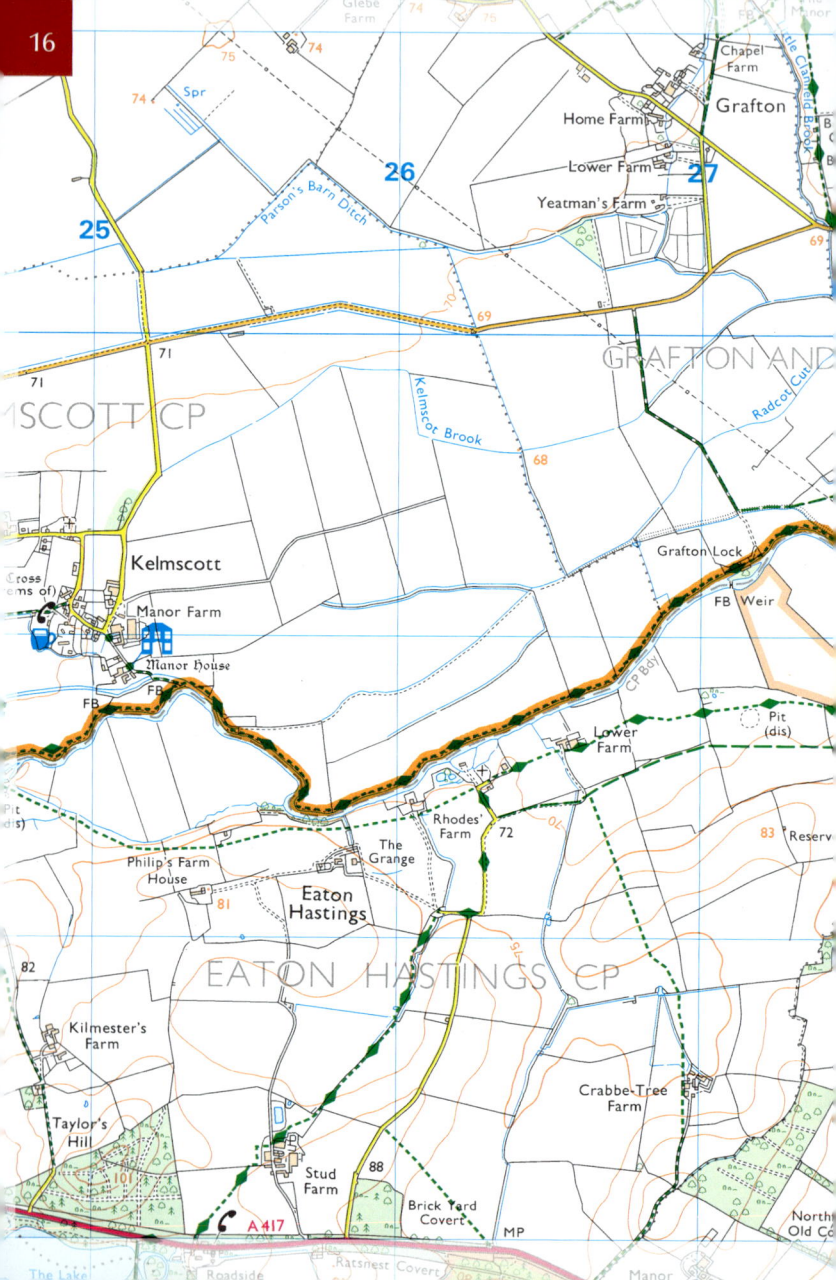

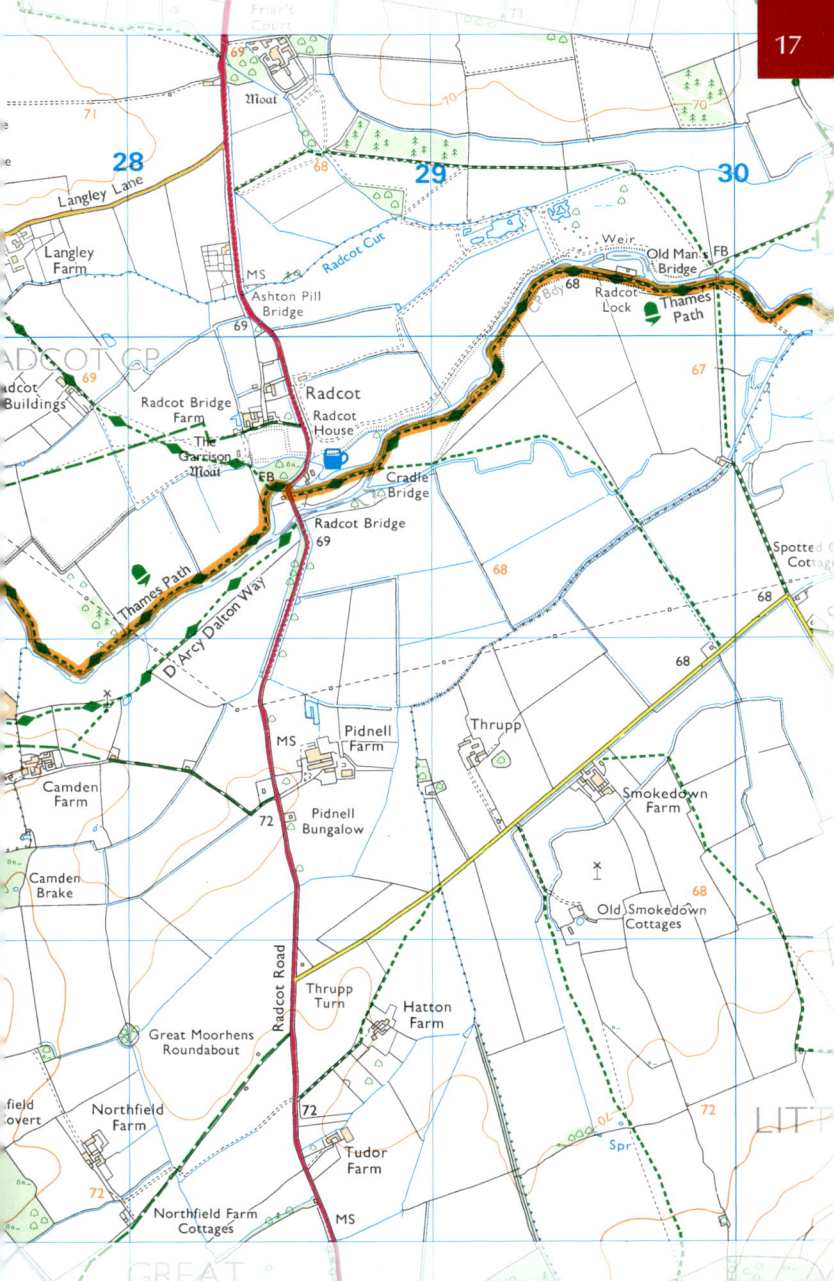

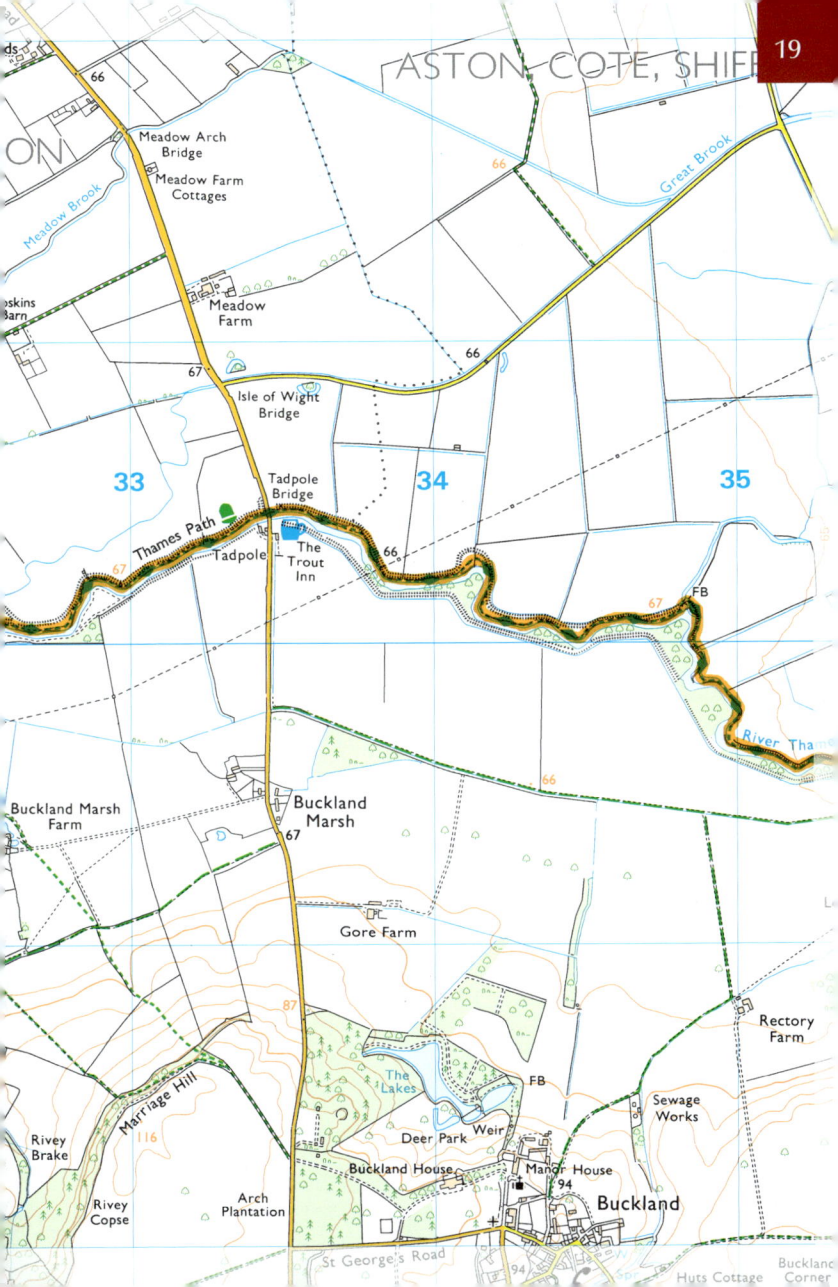

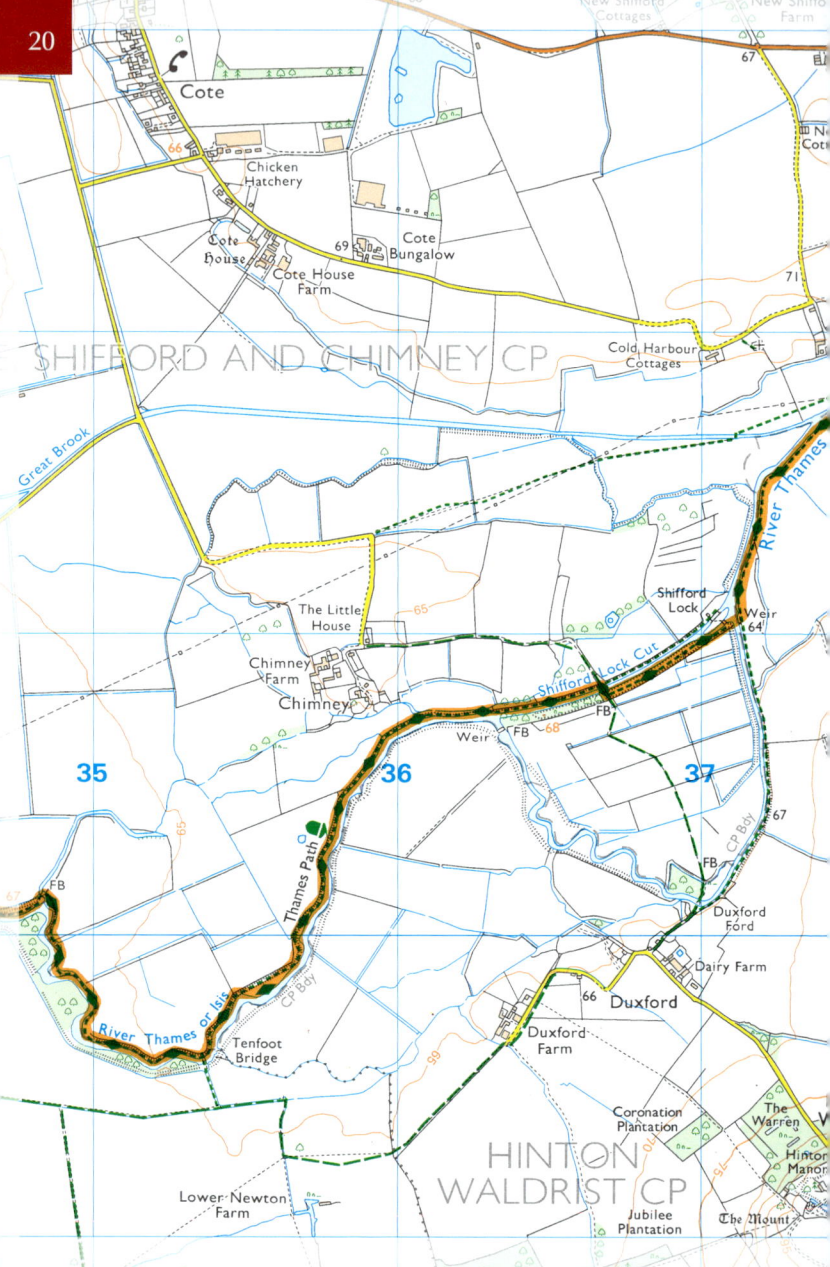

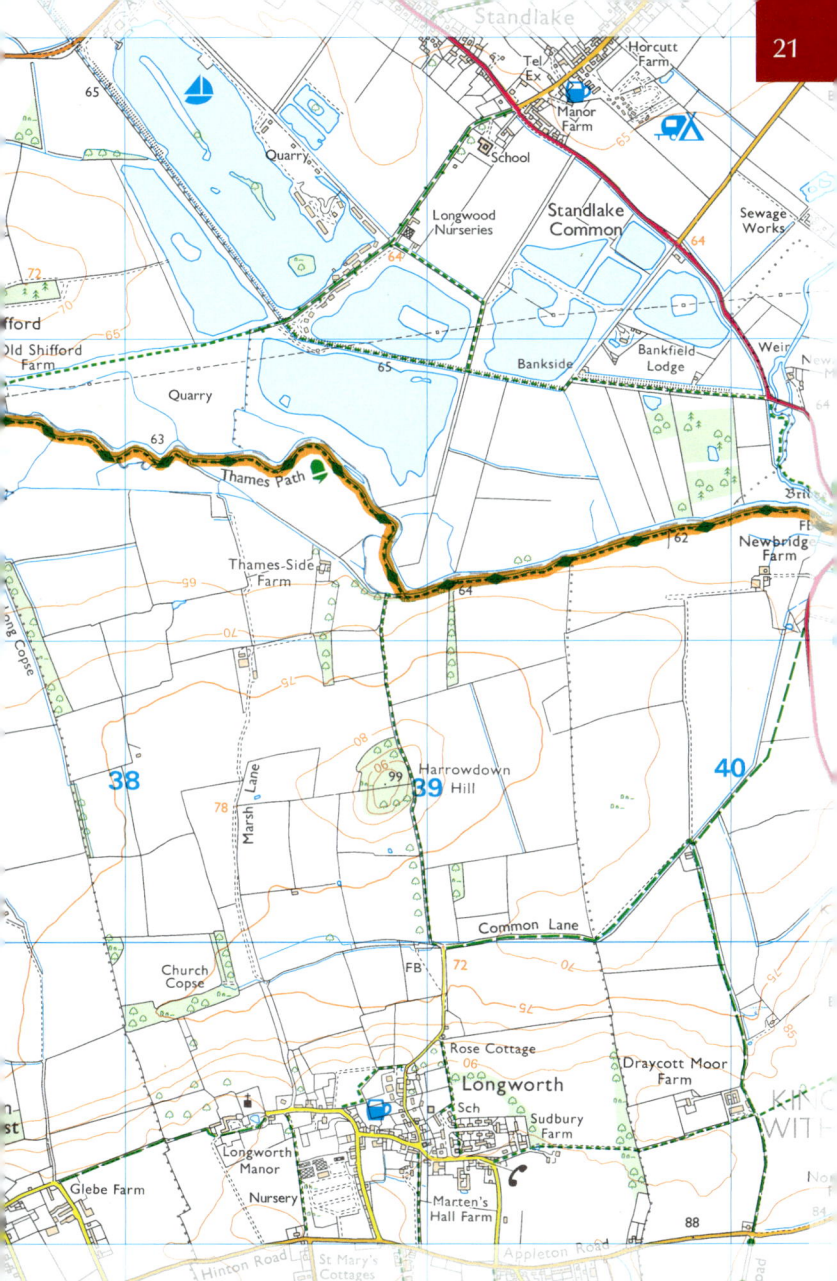

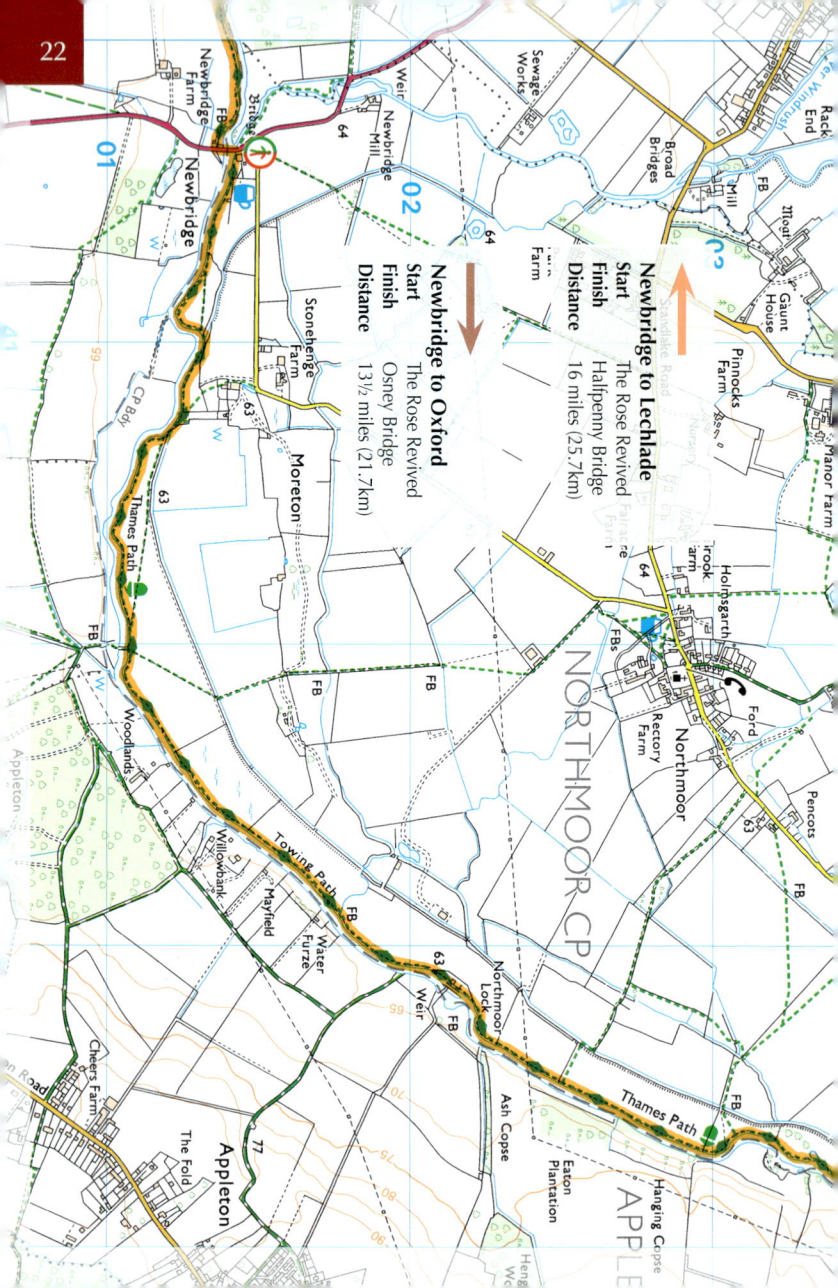

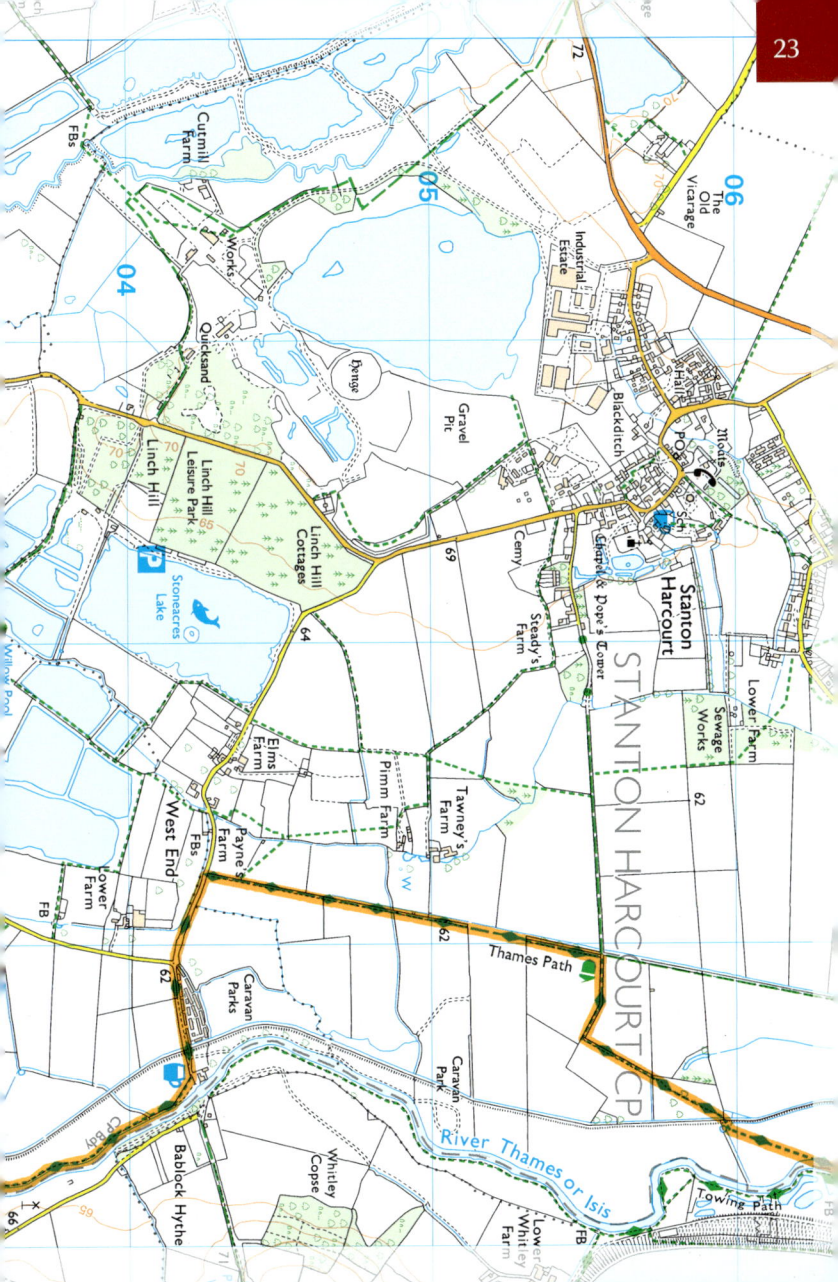

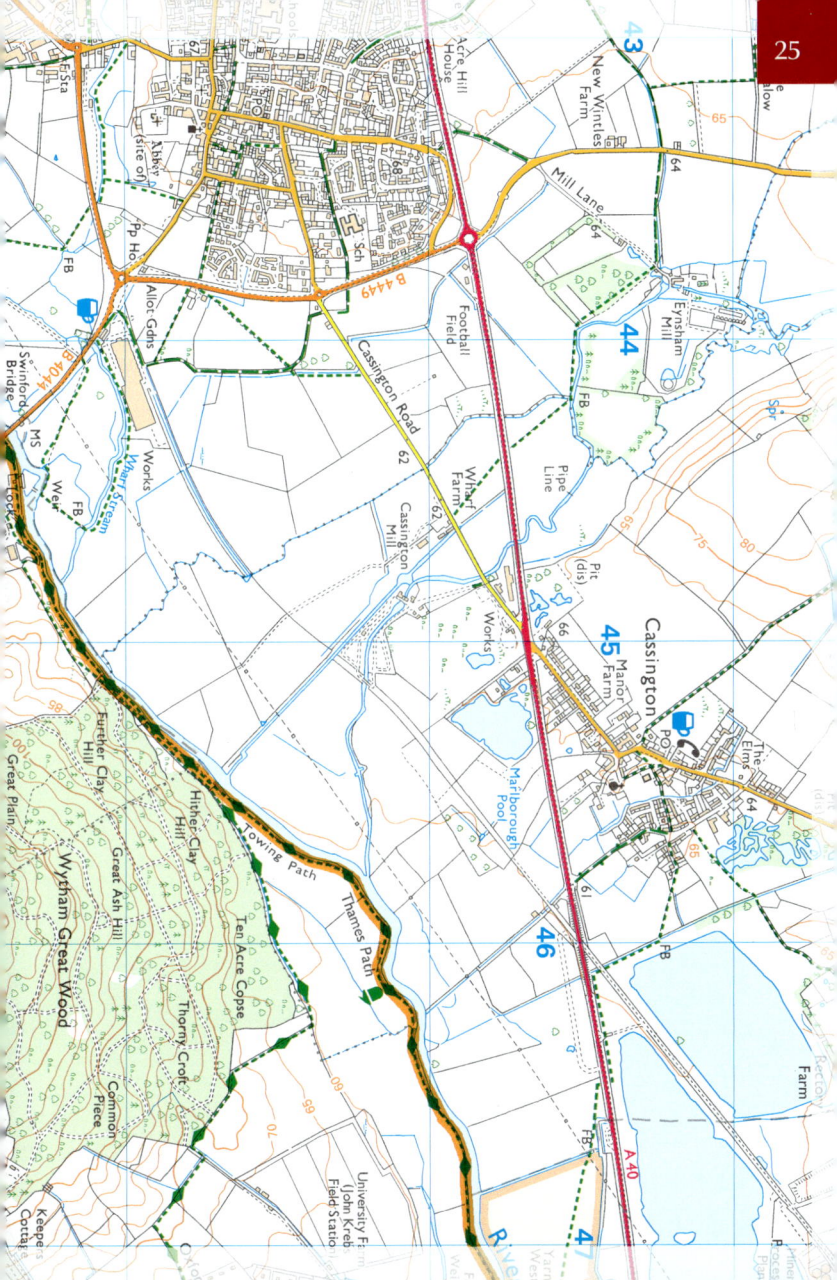

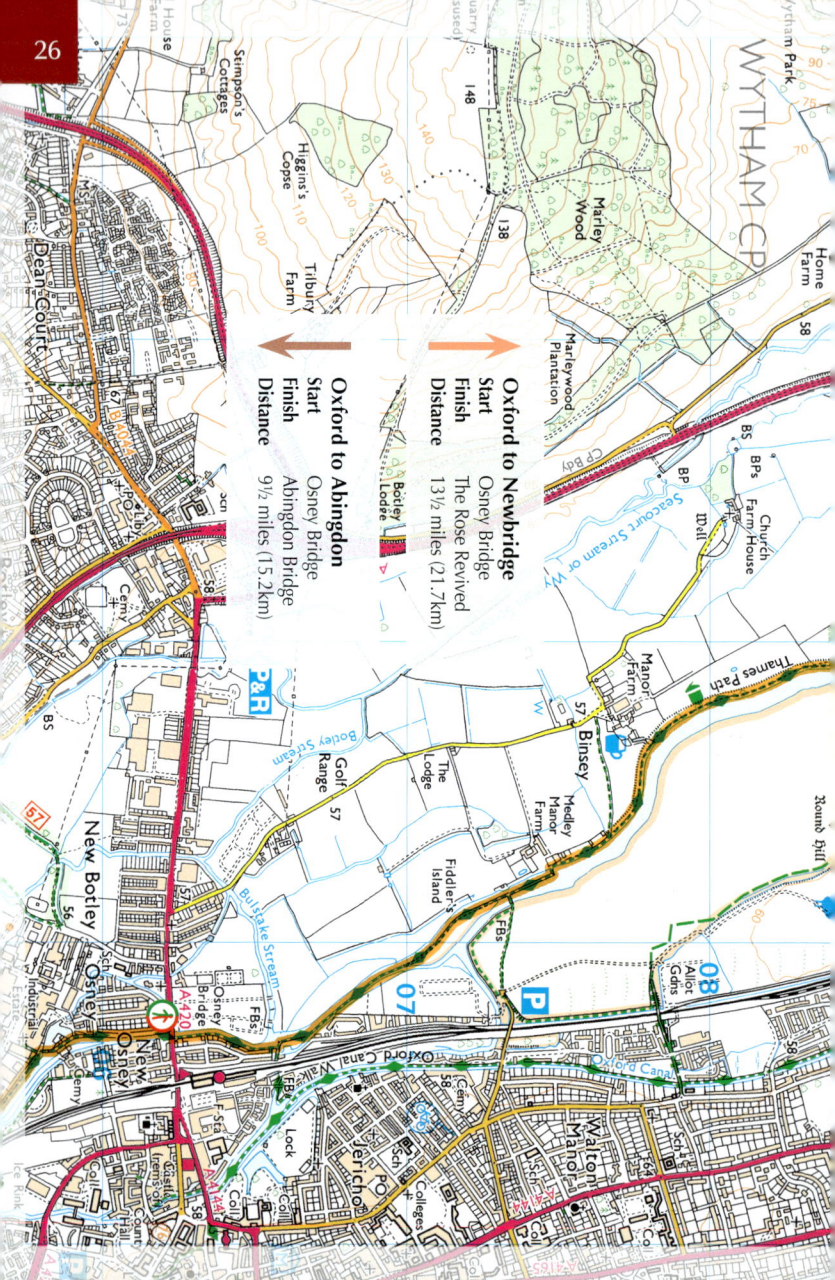

Oxford to Newbridge
Start: Osney Bridge
Finish: The Rose Revived
Distance: 13½ miles (21.7km)

Oxford to Abingdon
Start: Osney Bridge
Finish: Abingdon Bridge
Distance: 9½ miles (15.2km)

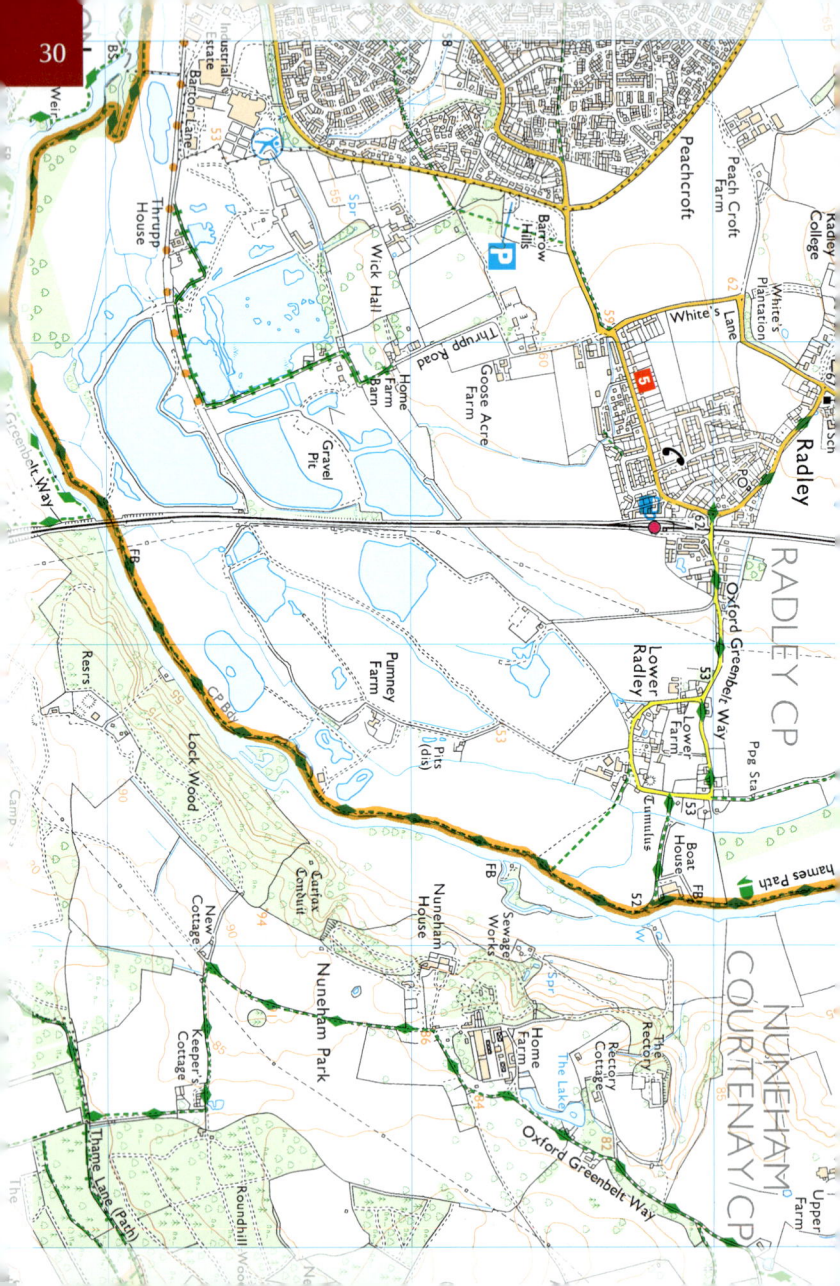

Abingdon to Oxford
Start Abingdon Bridge
Finish Osney Bridge
Distance 9½ miles (15.2km)

Abingdon to Dorchester
Start Abingdon Bridge
Finish River Thame/Thames confluence (SU 577 932)
Distance 9 miles (14.5km)

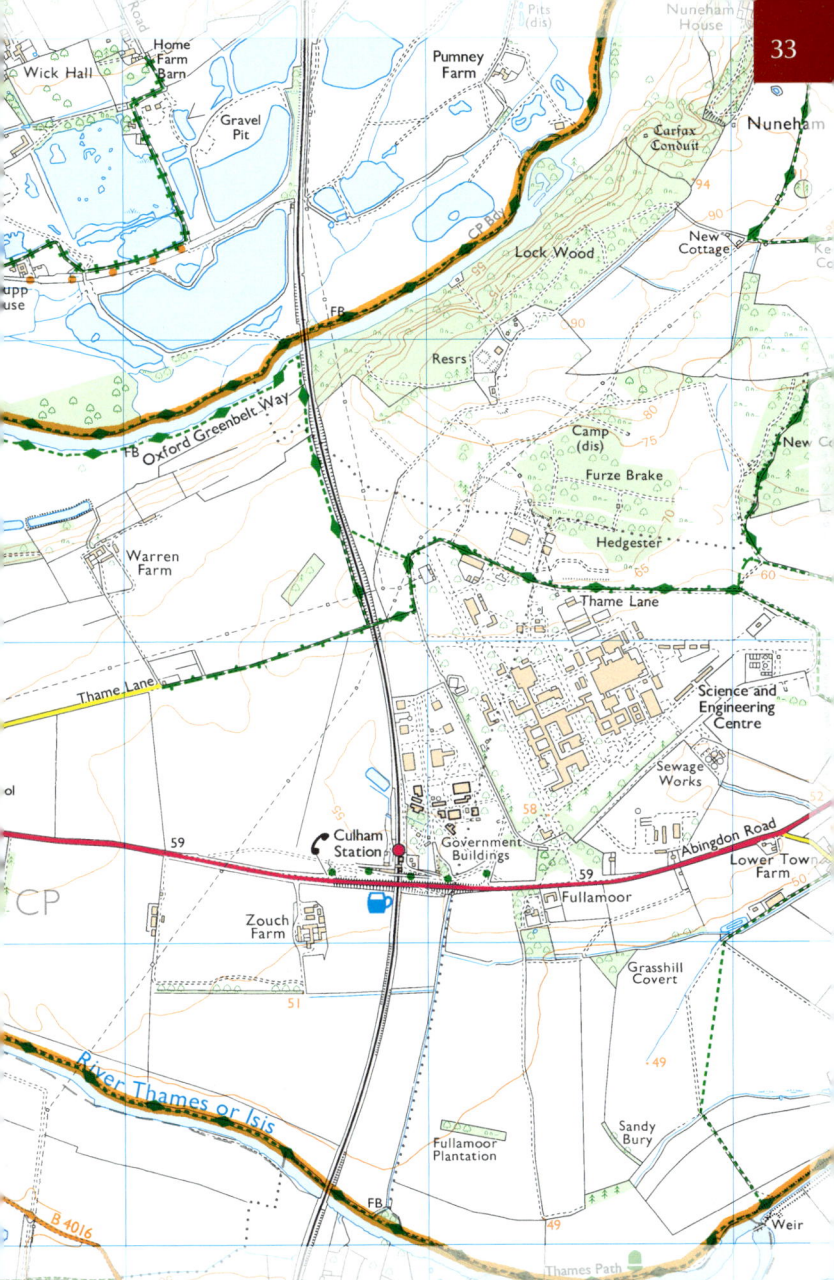

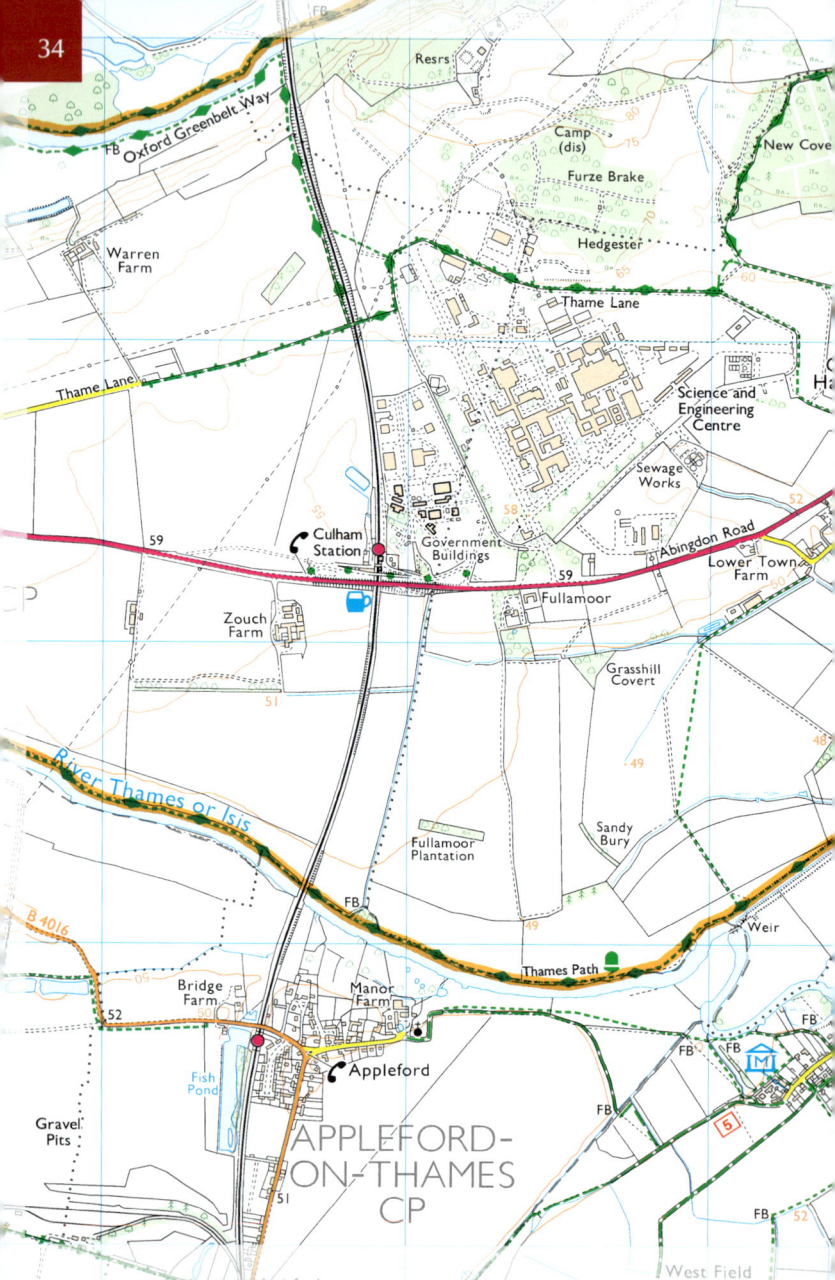

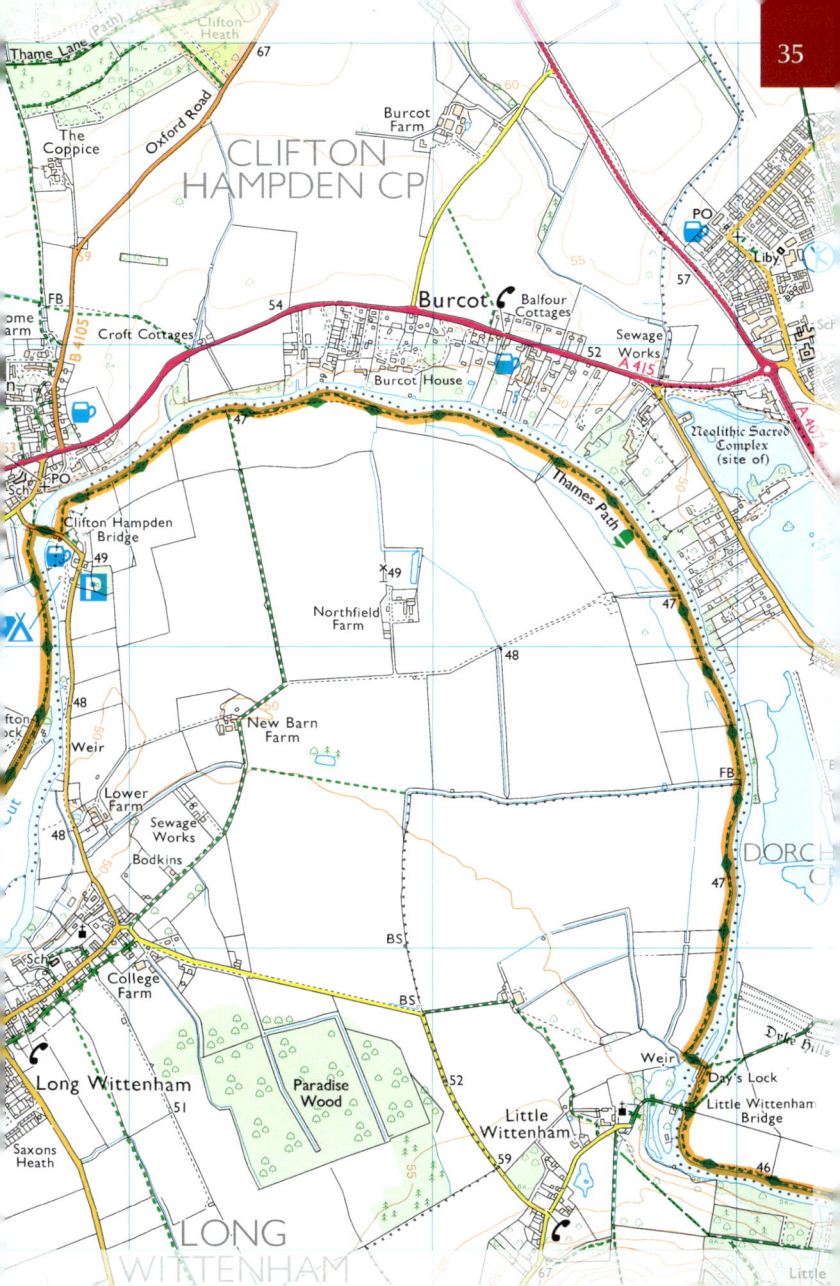

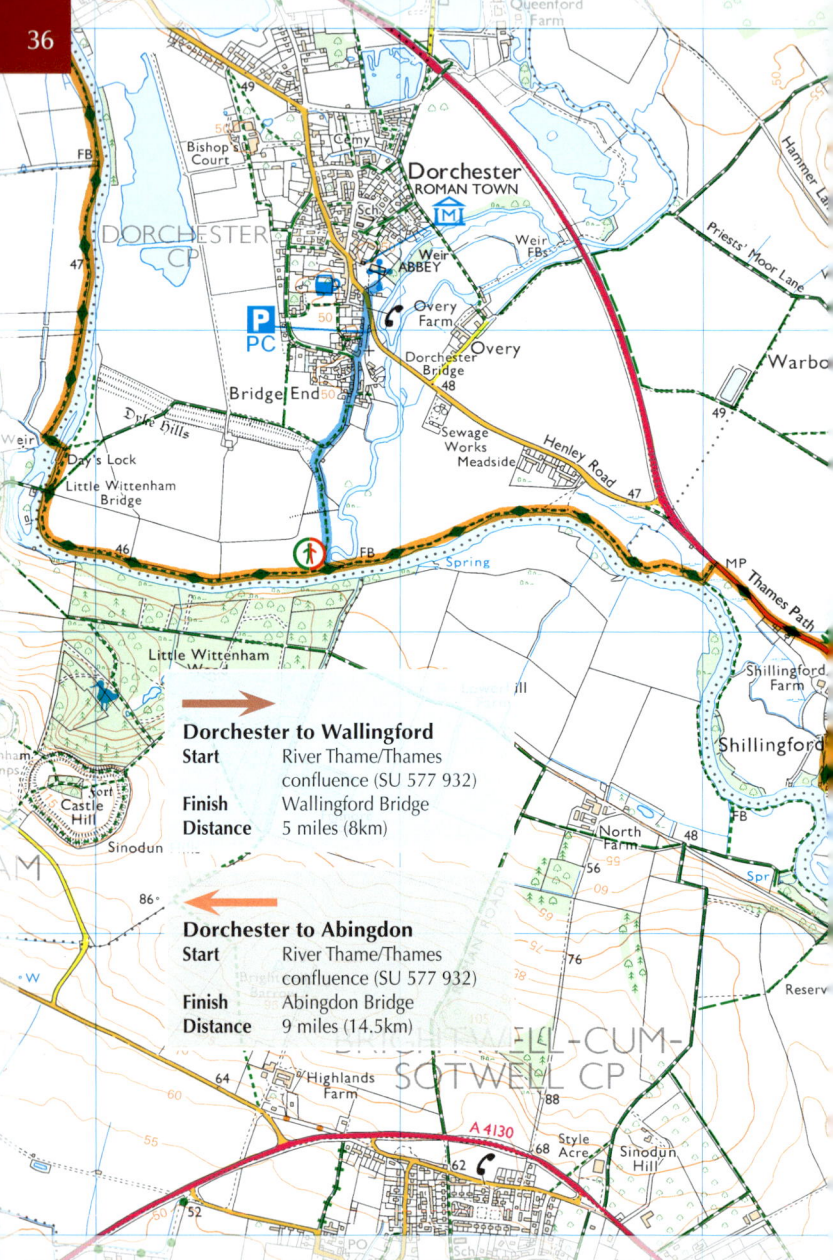

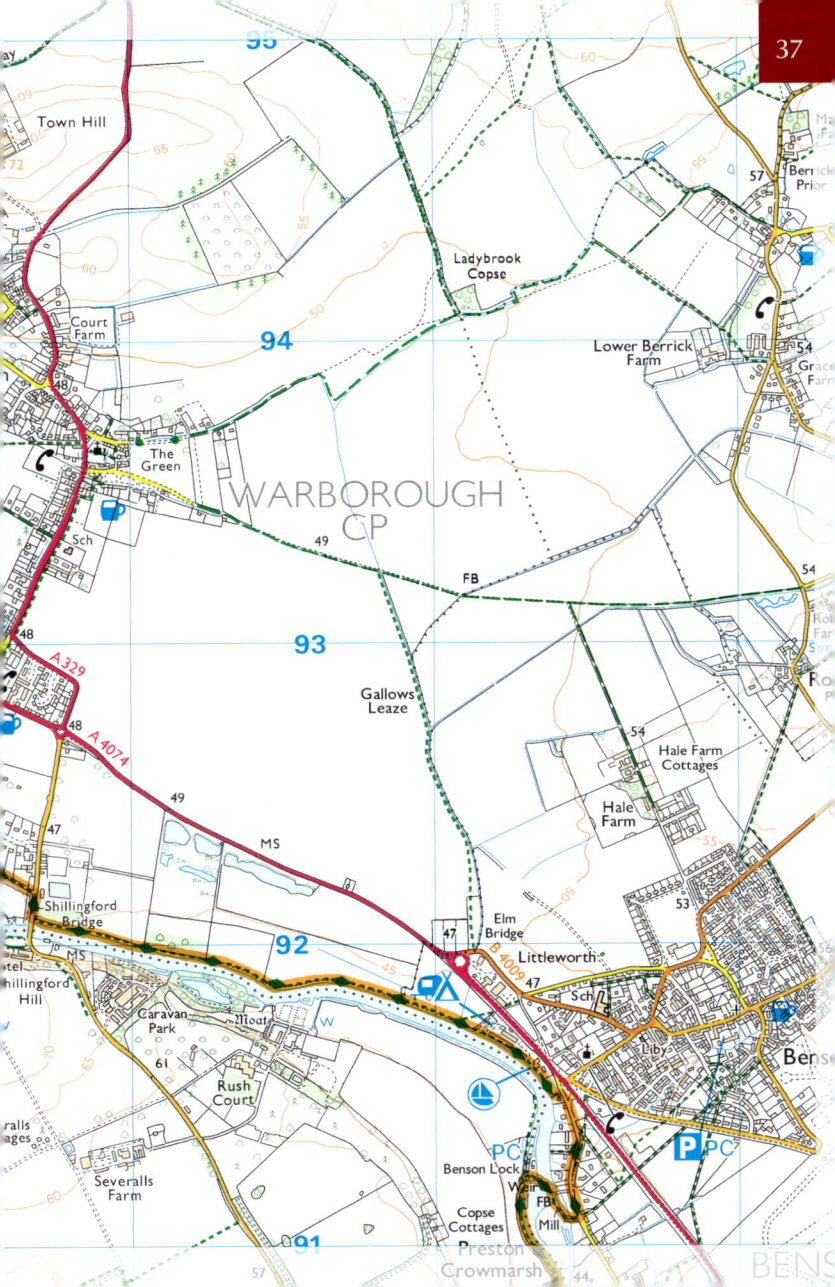

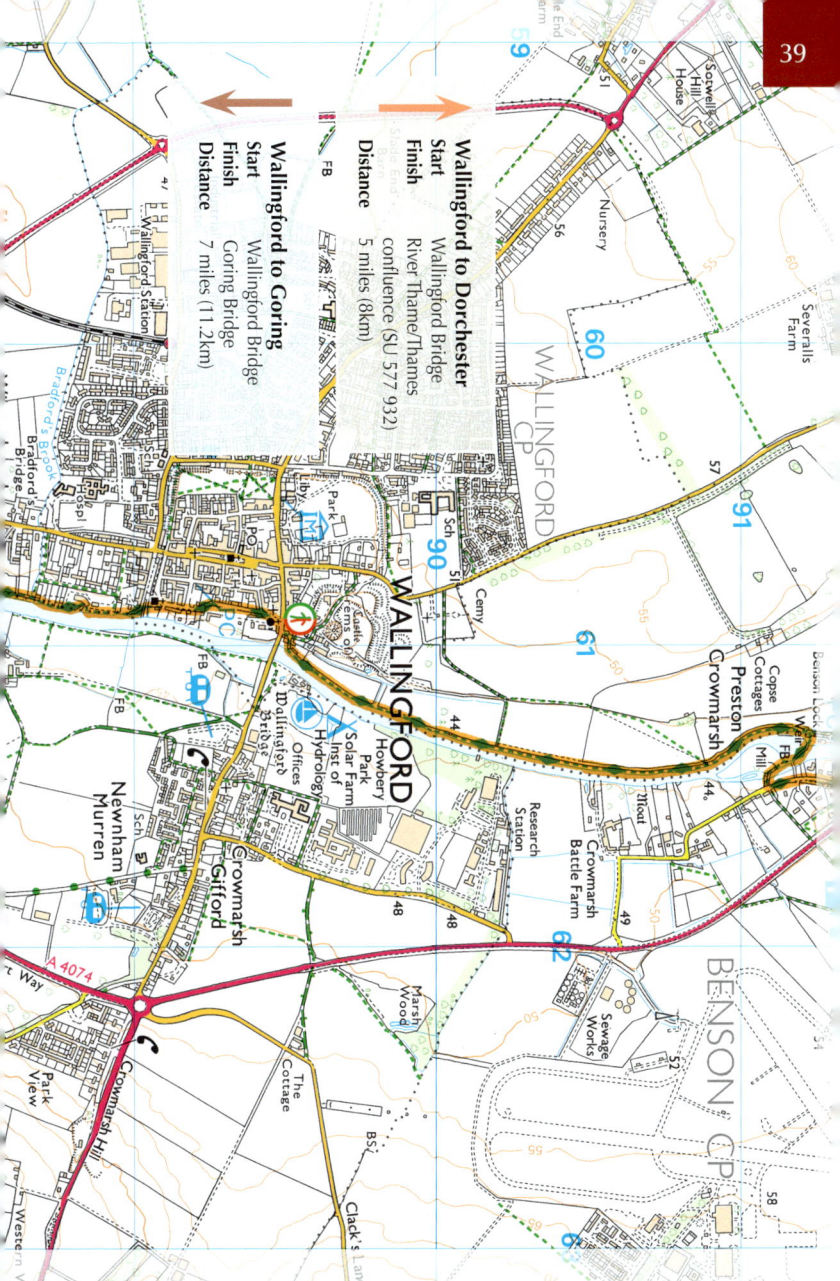

Wallingford to Dorchester
Start Wallingford Bridge
Finish River Thame/Thames confluence (SU 577 932)
Distance 5 miles (8km)

Wallingford to Goring
Start Wallingford Bridge
Finish Goring Bridge
Distance 7 miles (11.2km)

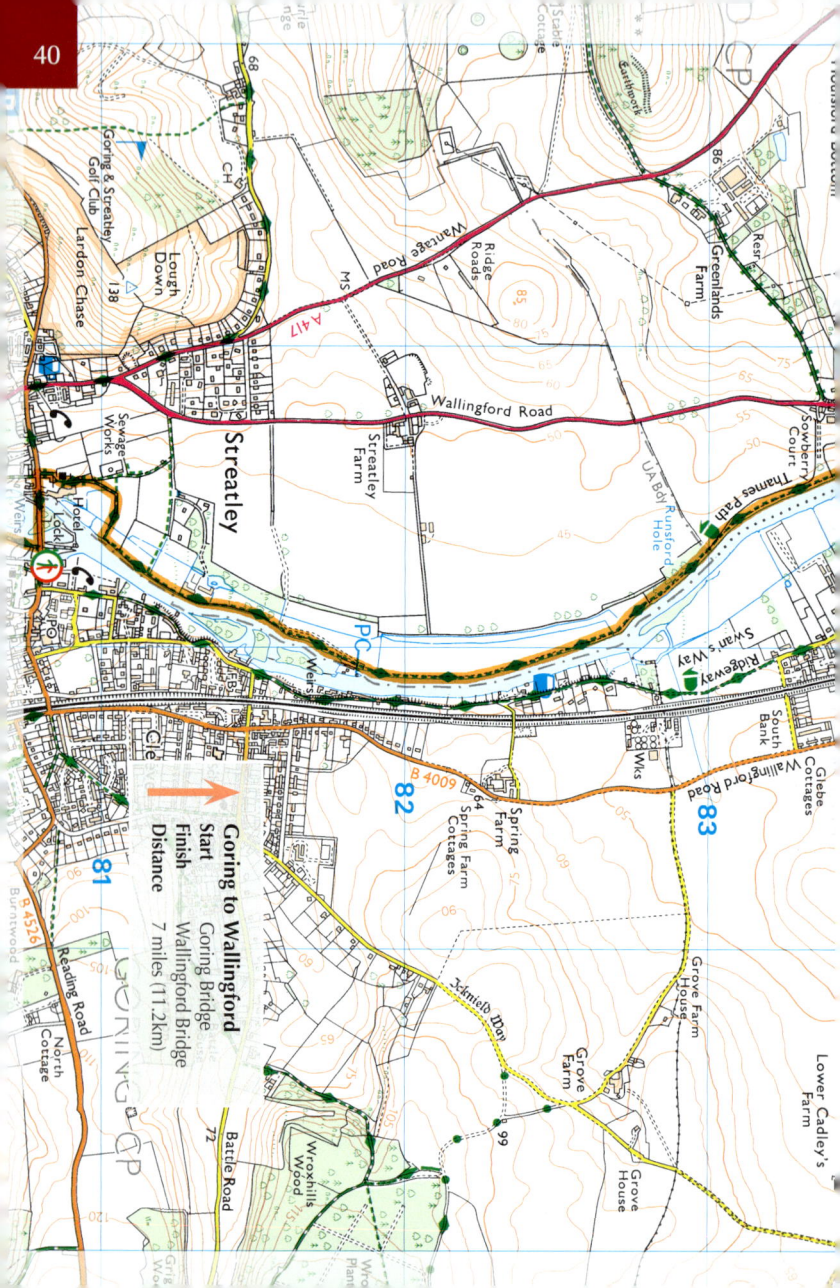

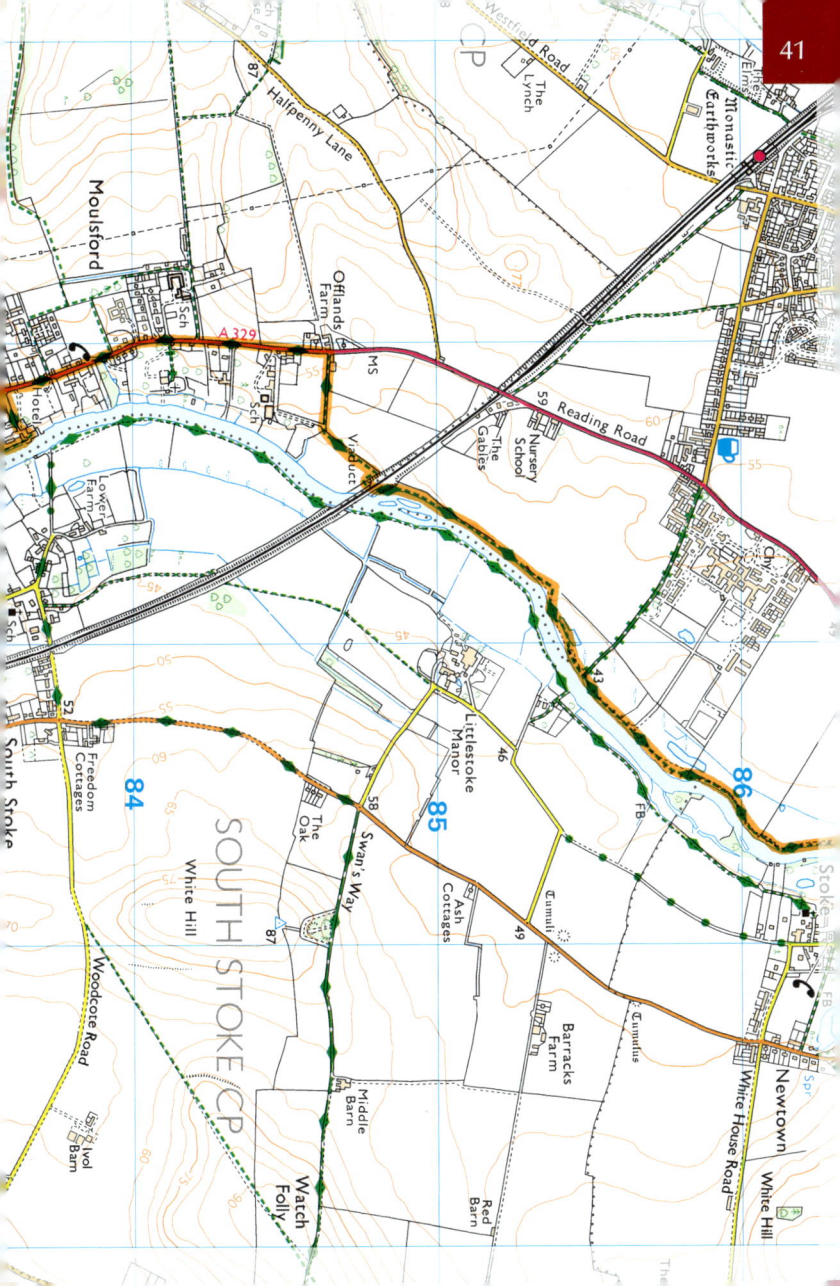

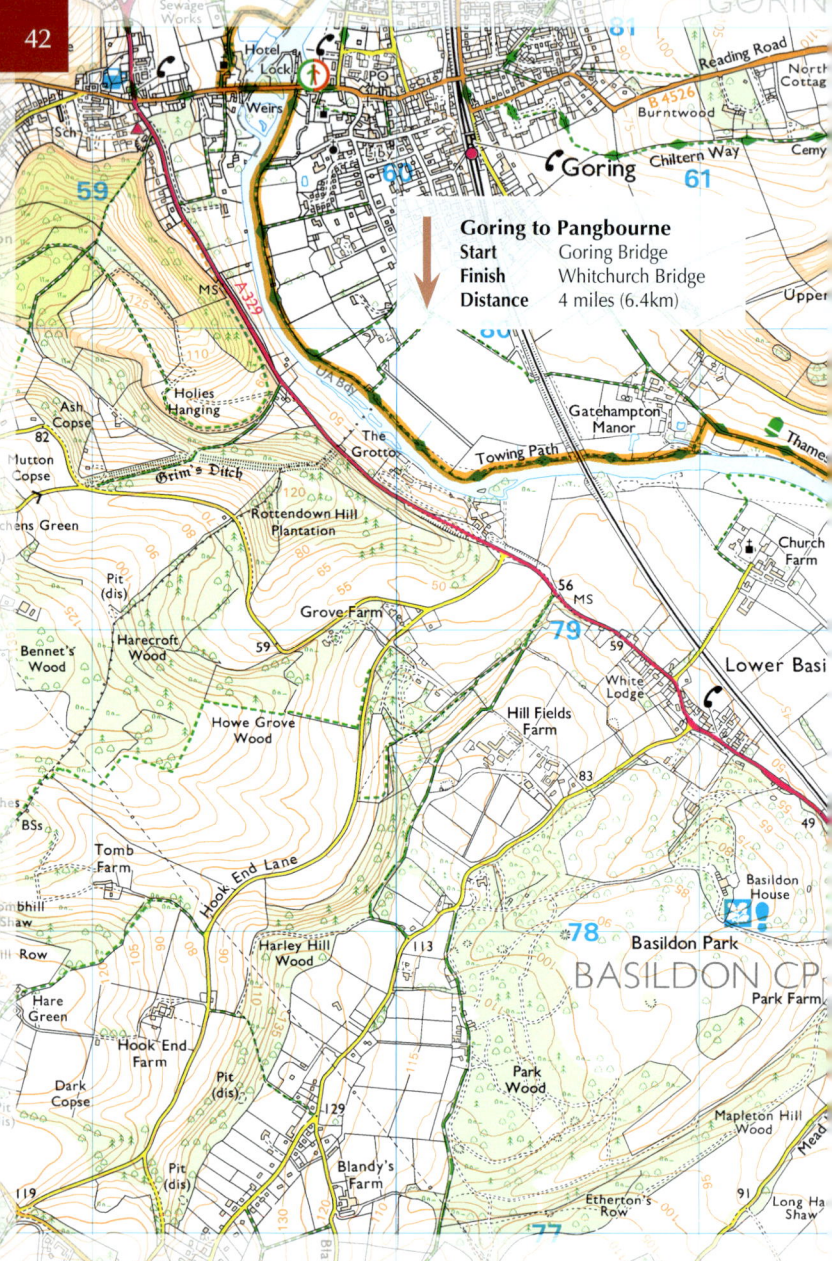

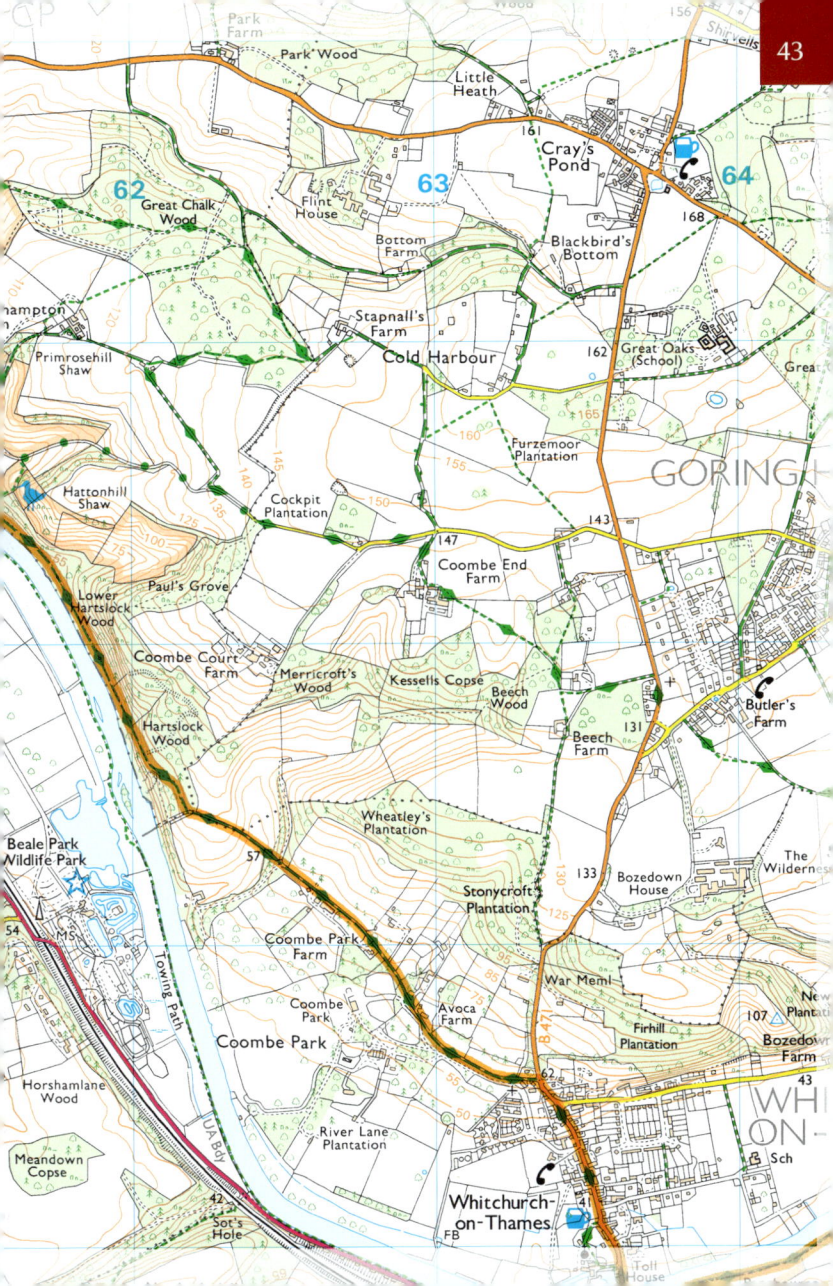

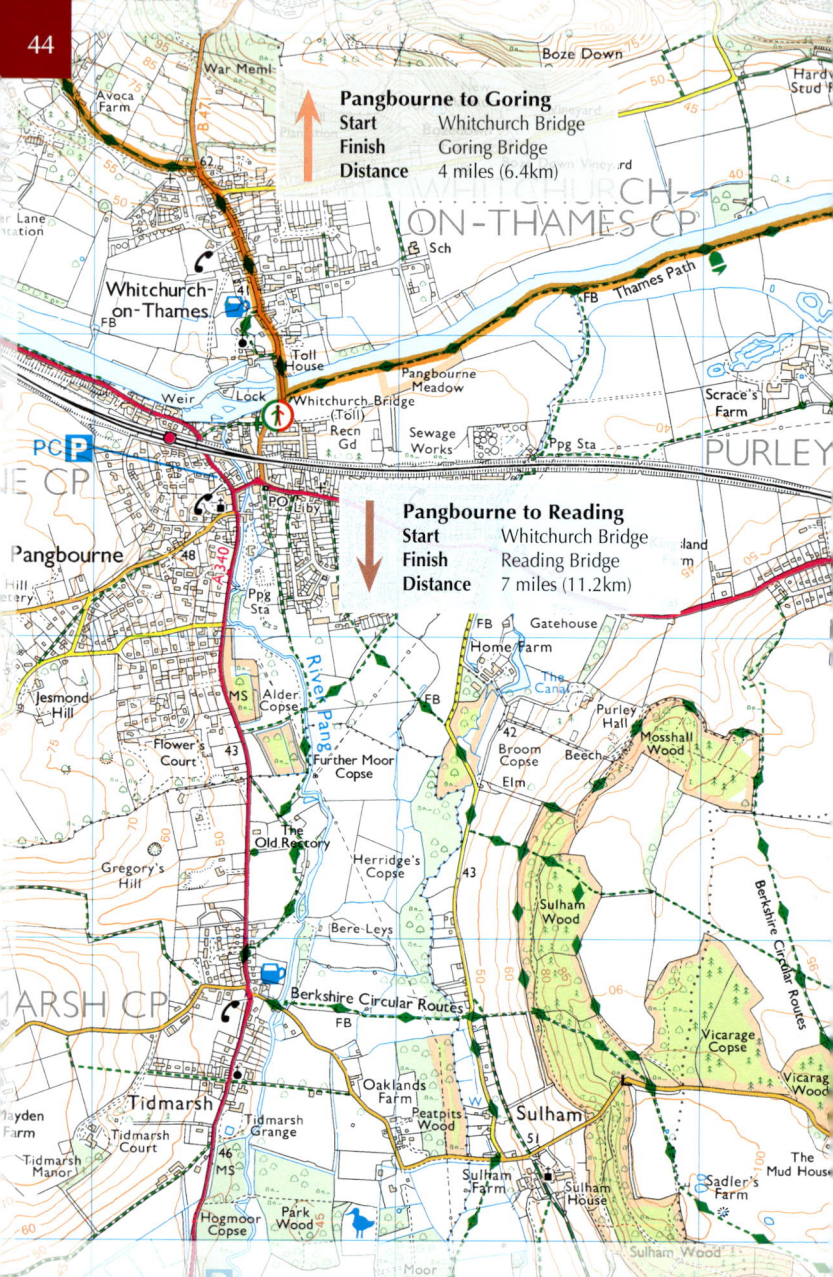

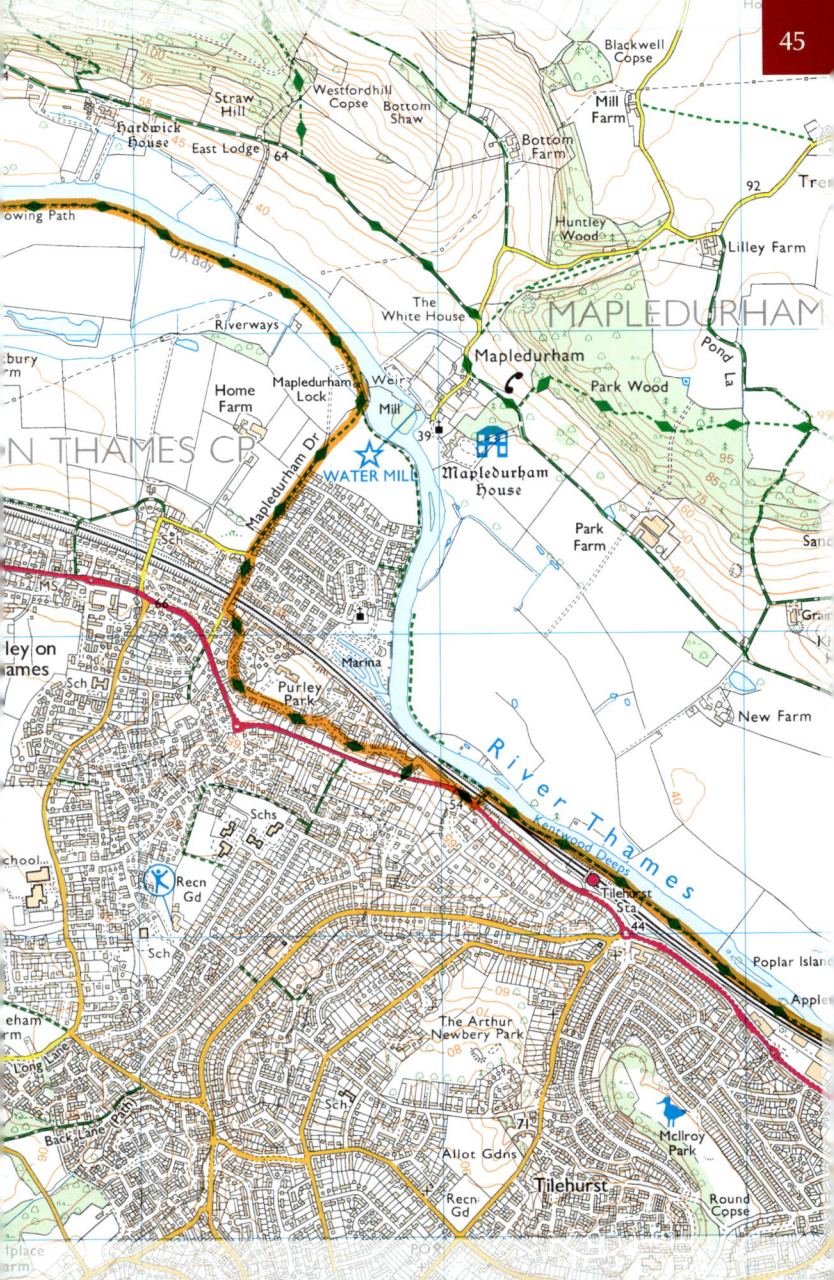

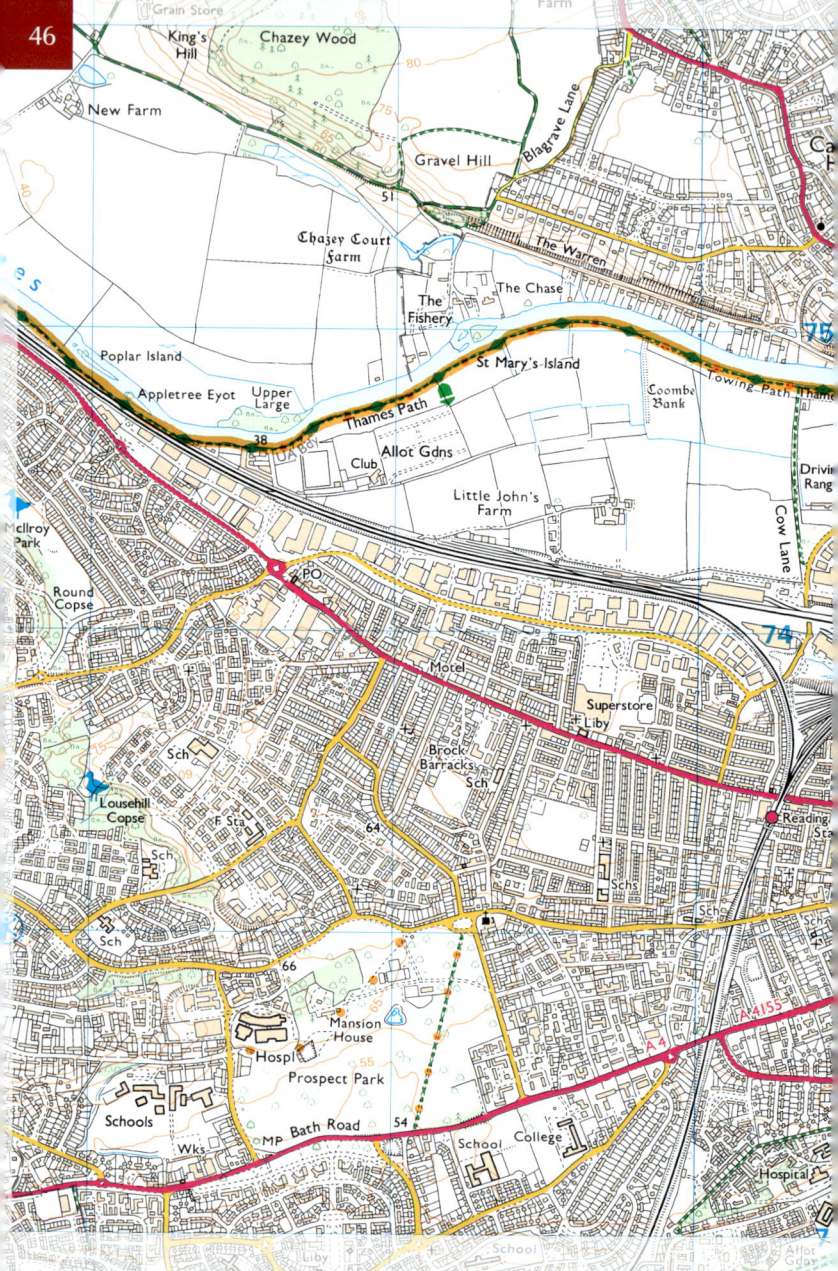

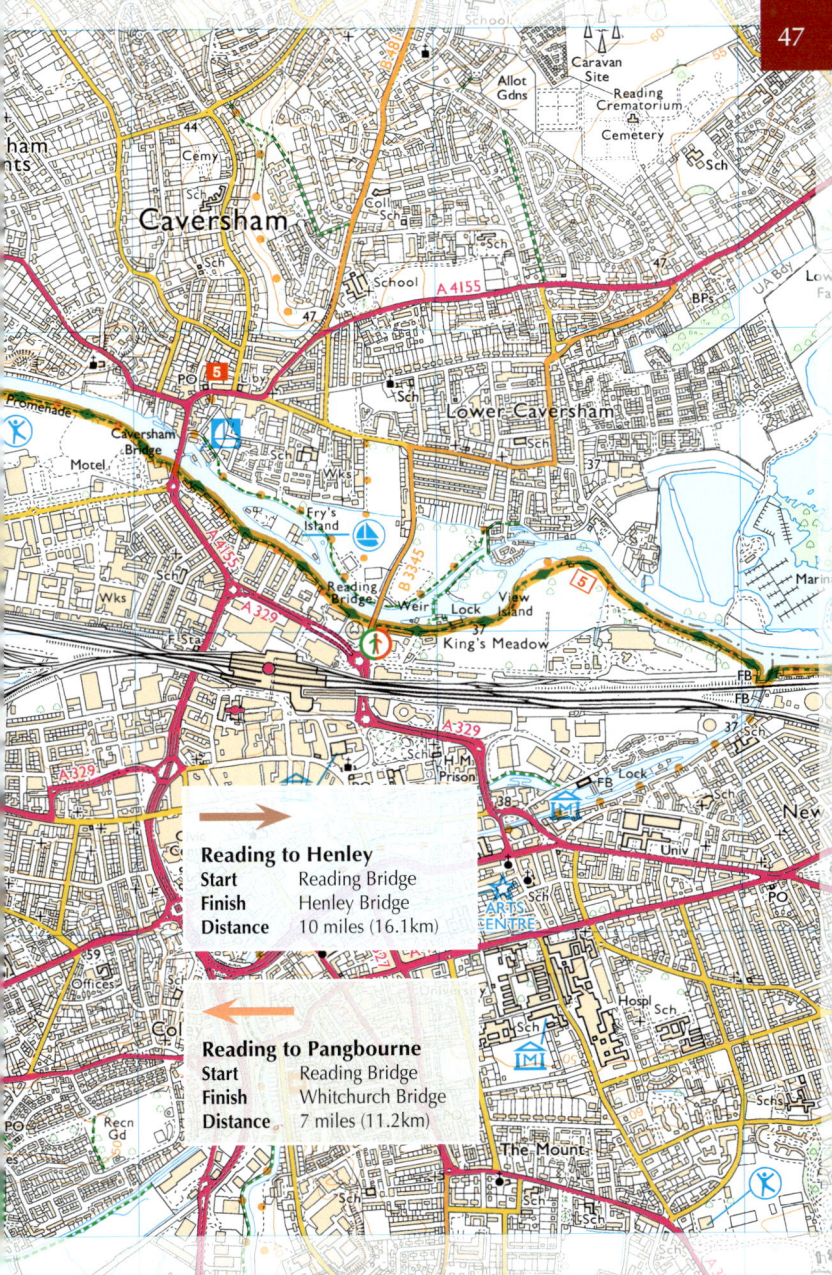

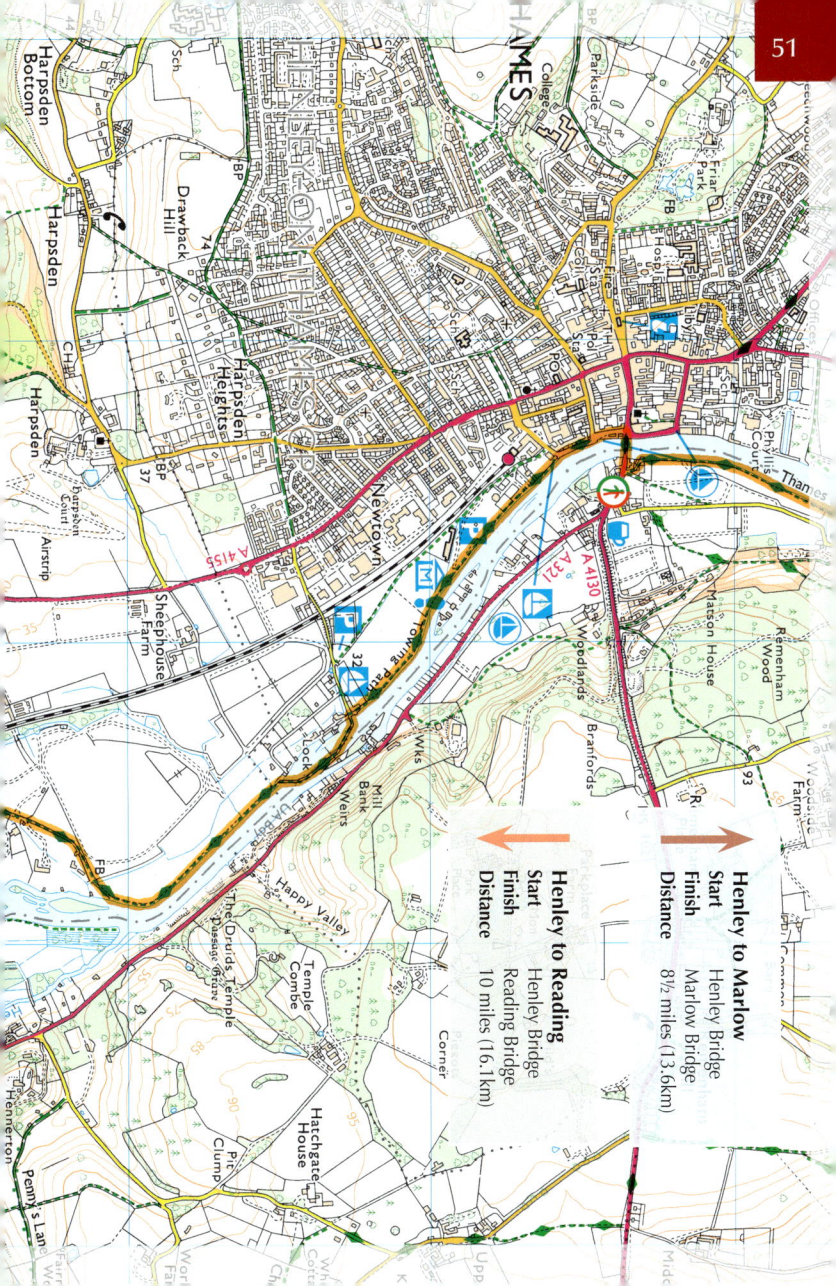

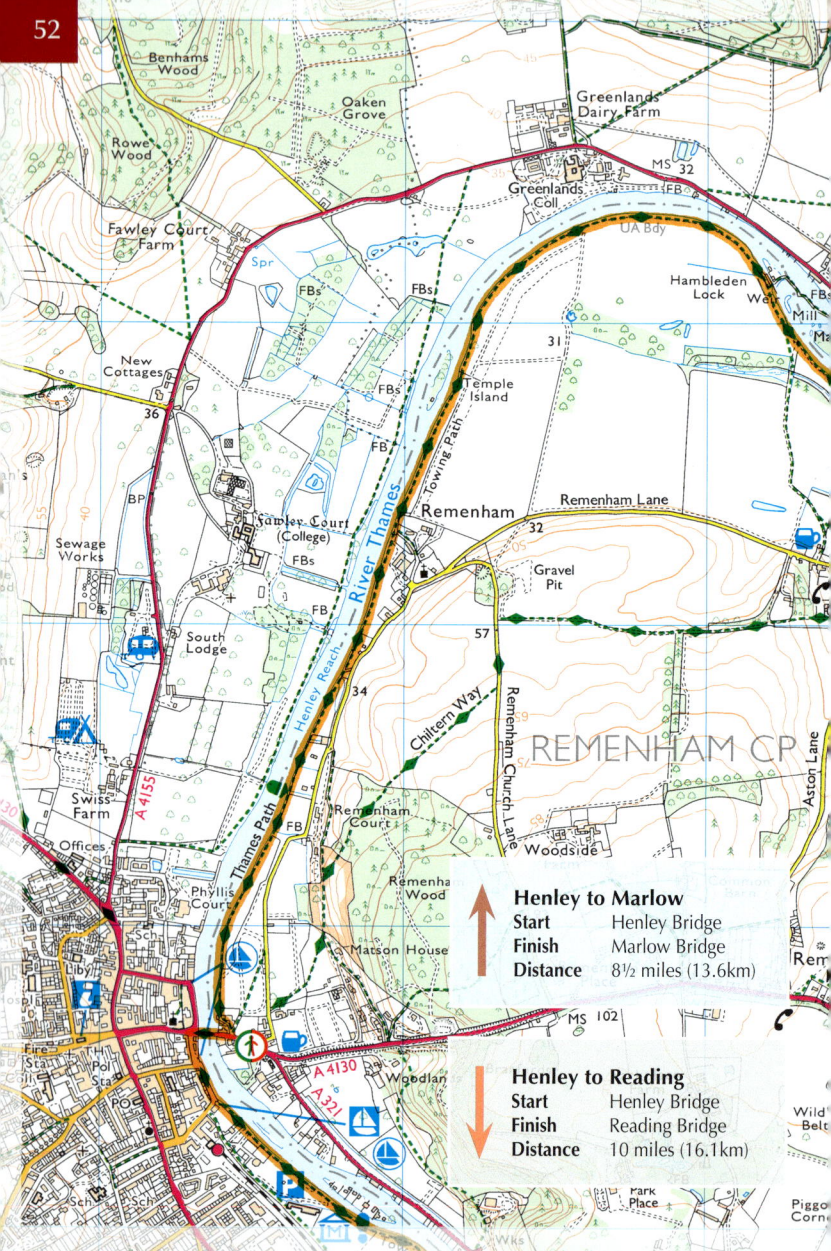

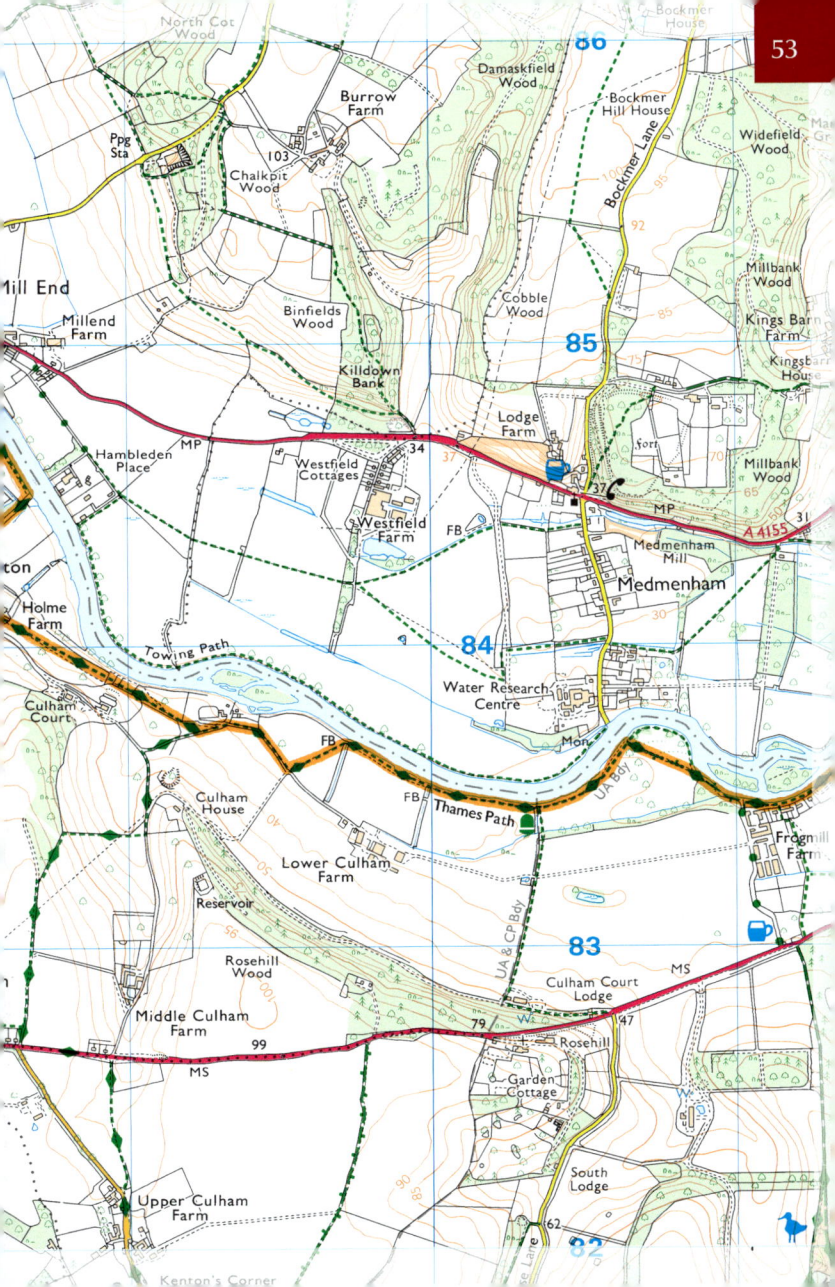

54

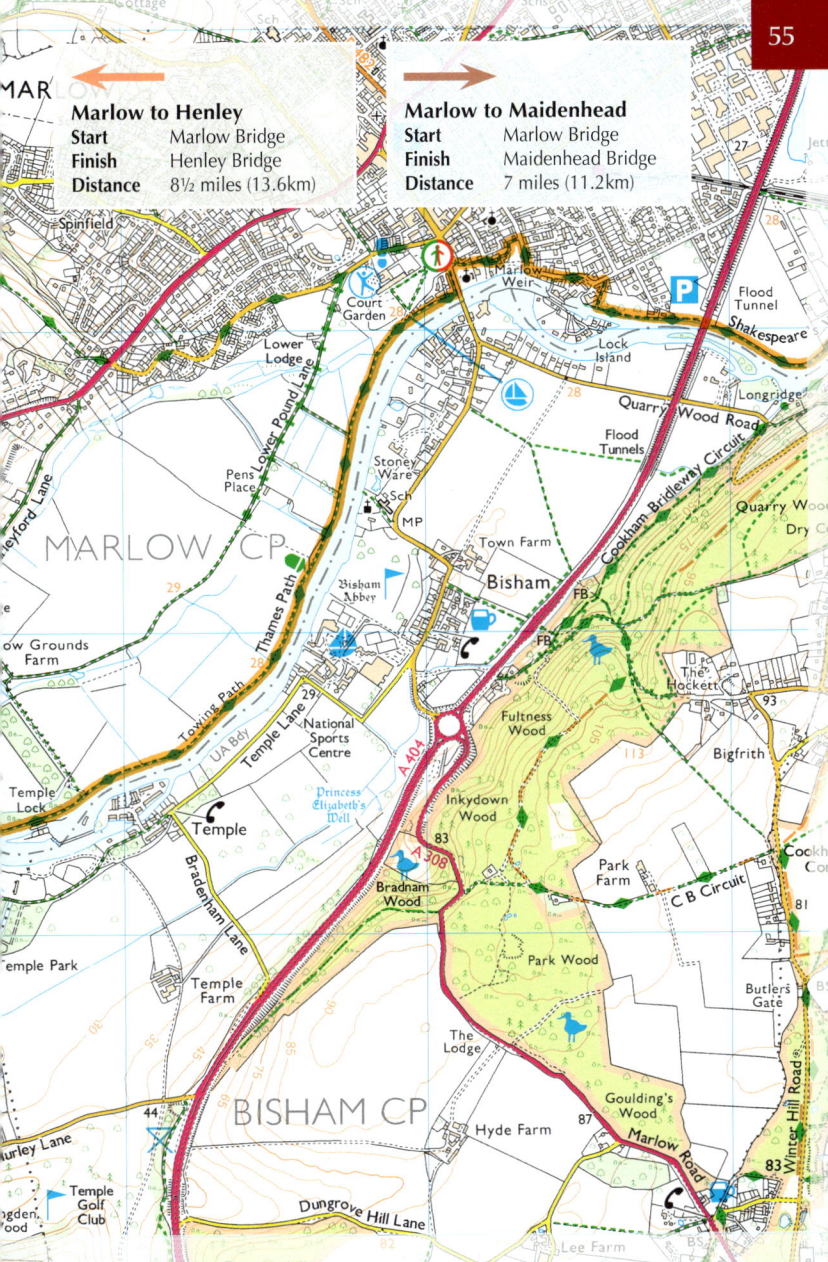

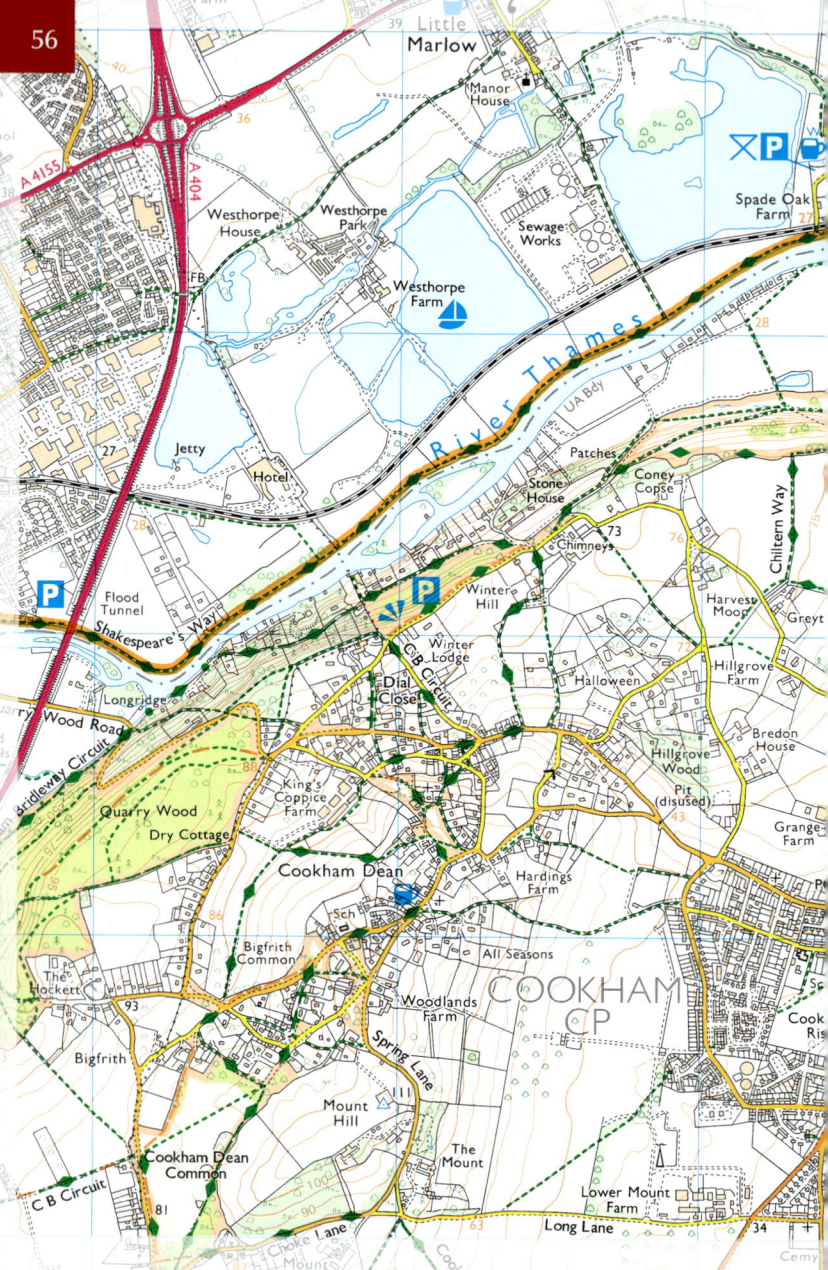

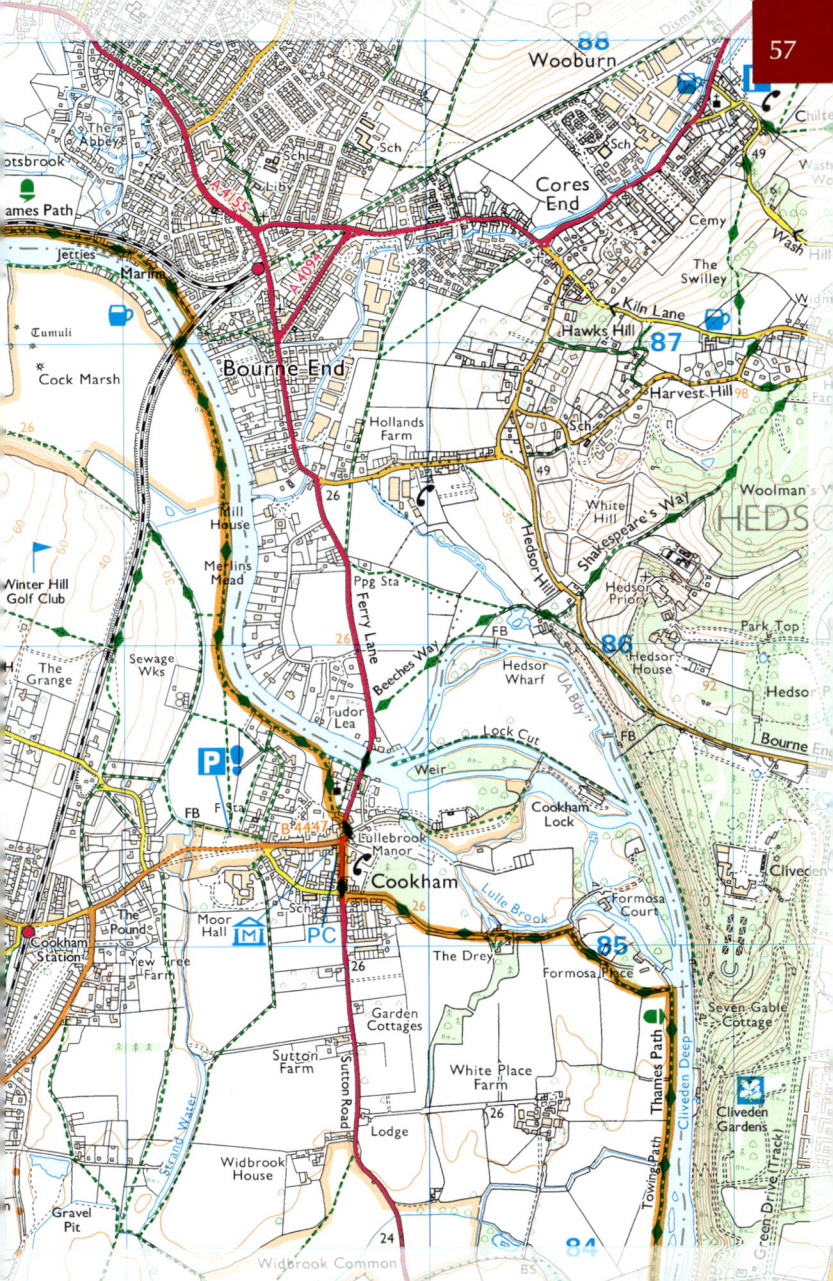

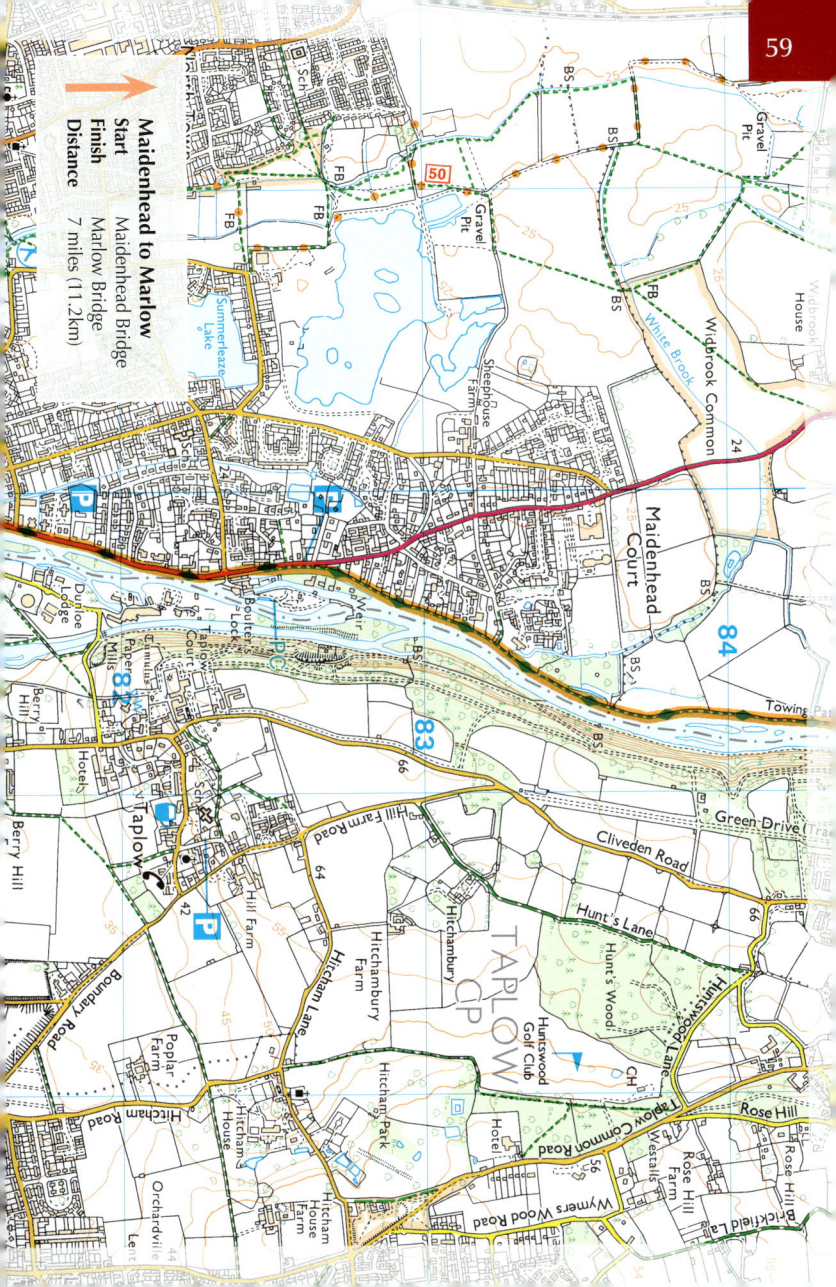

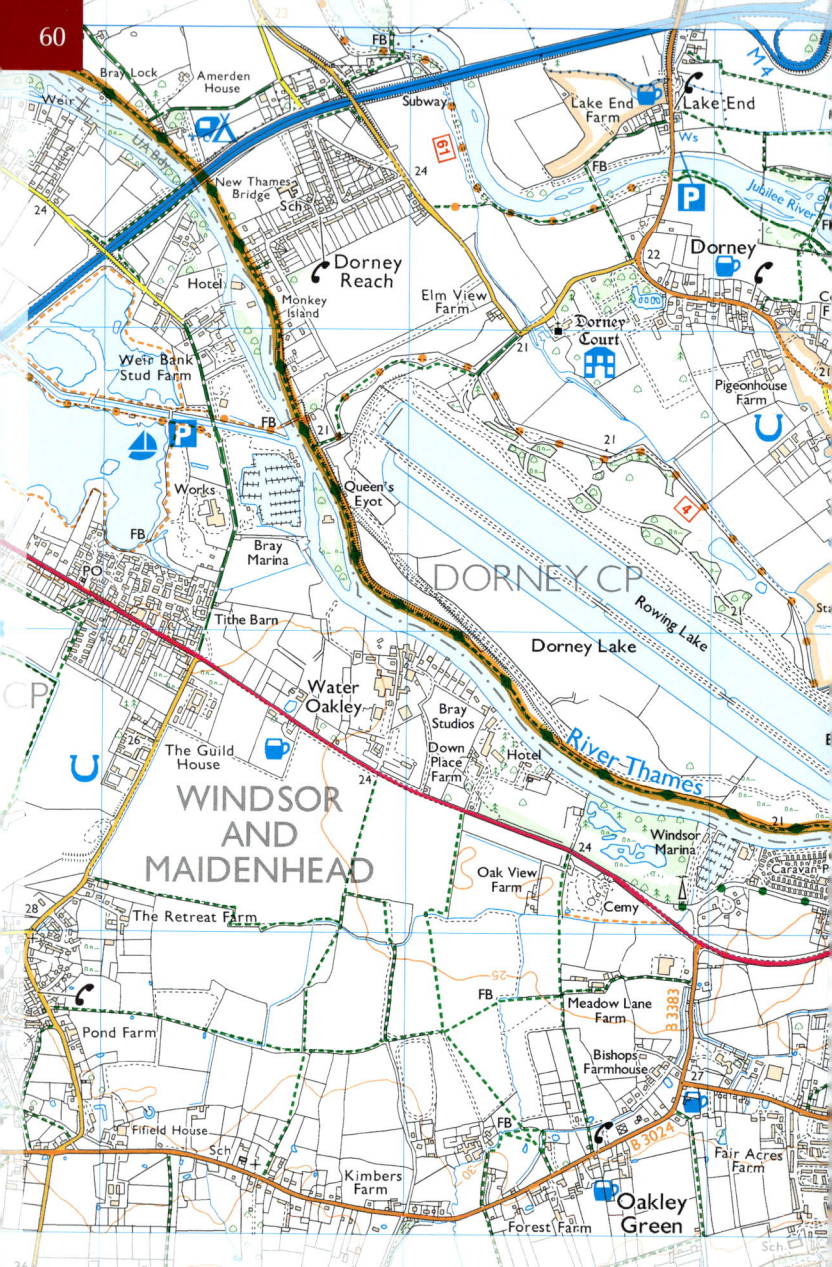

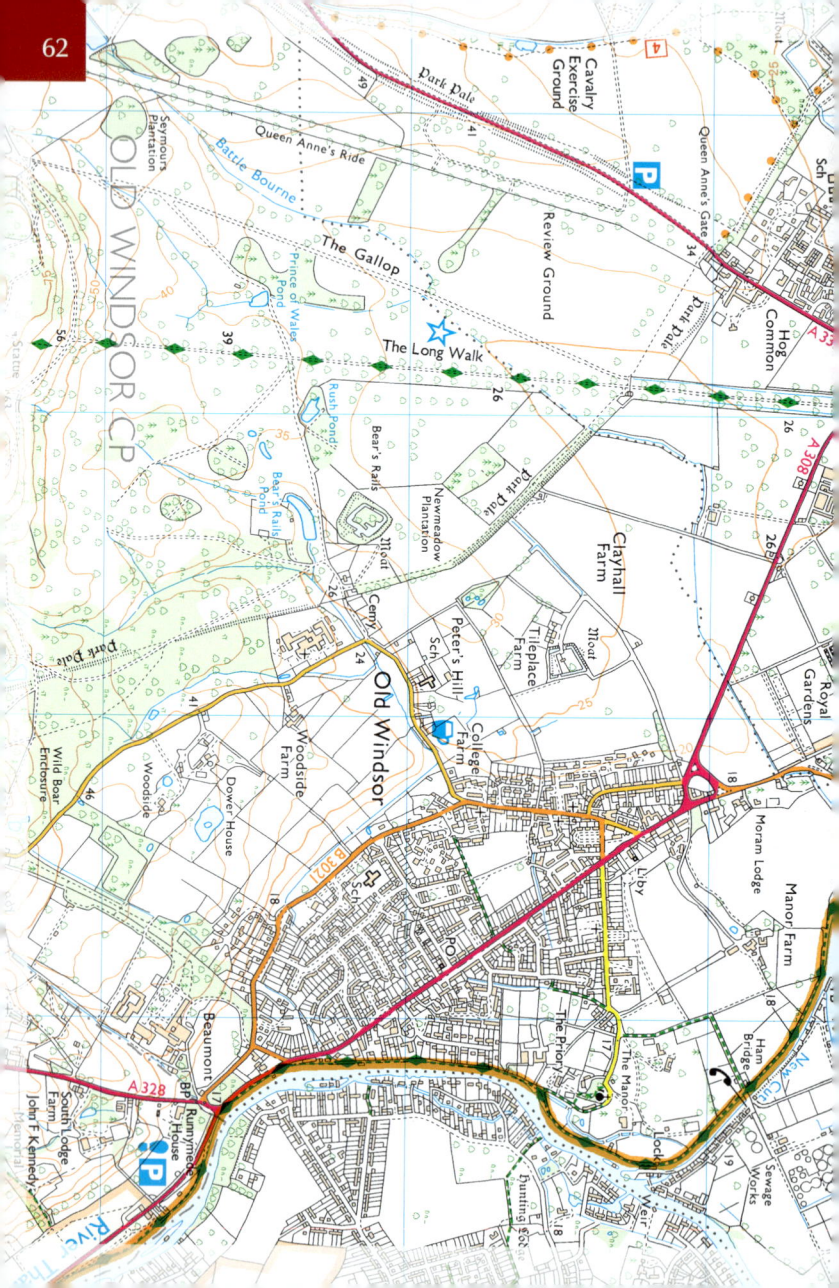

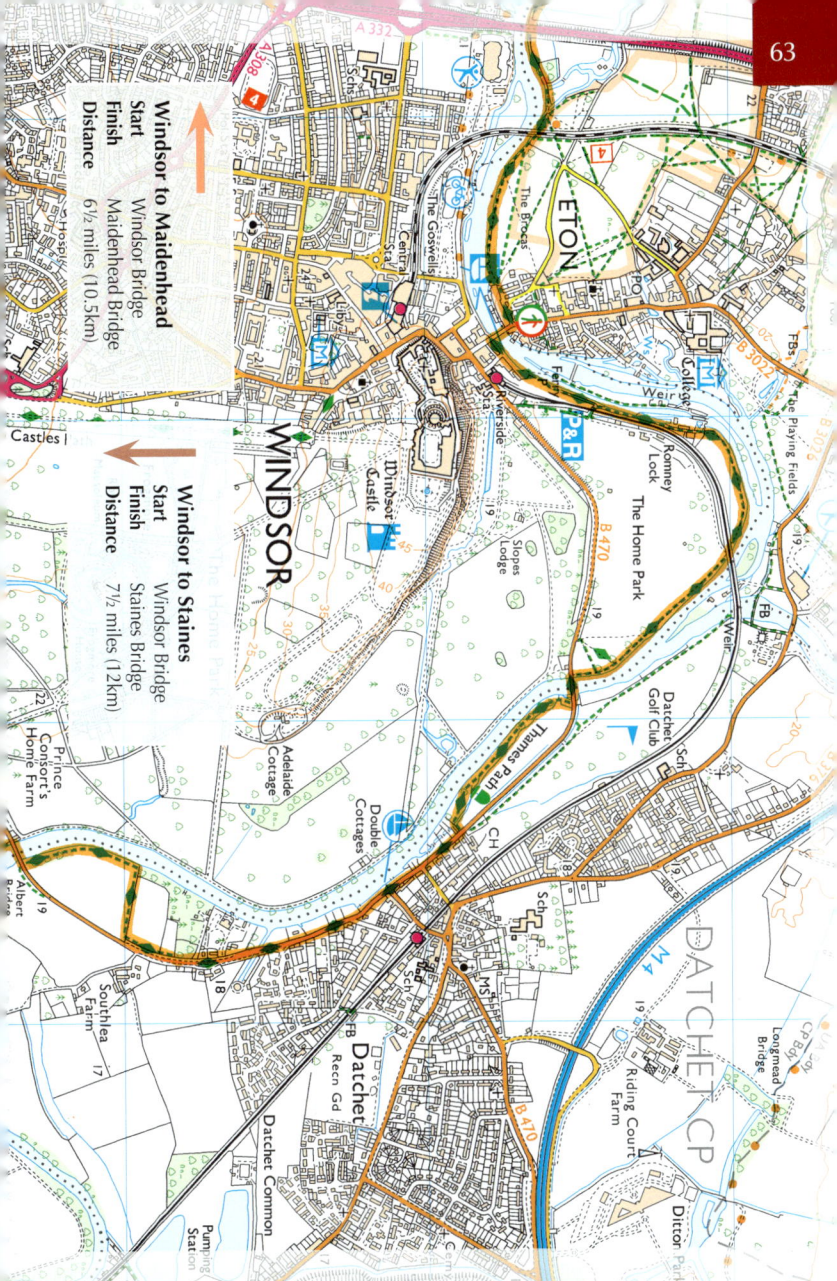

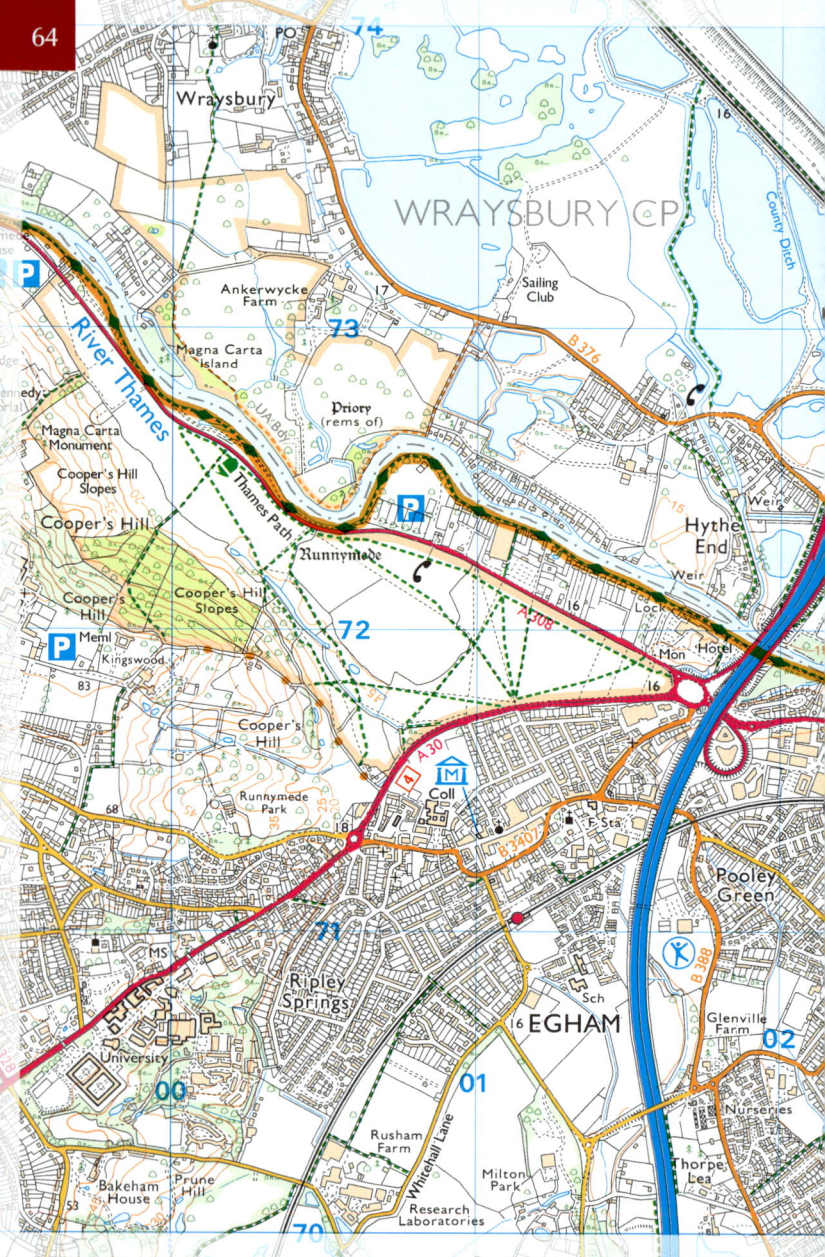

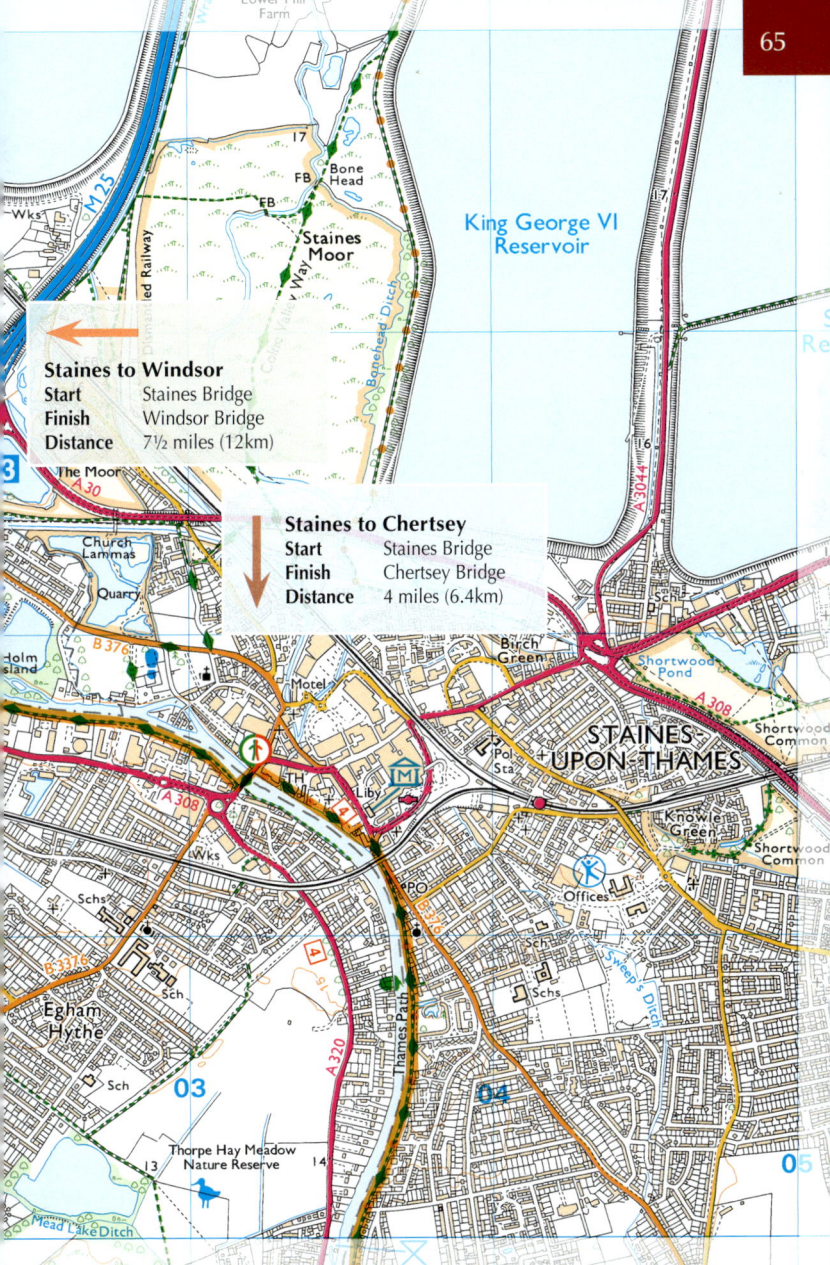

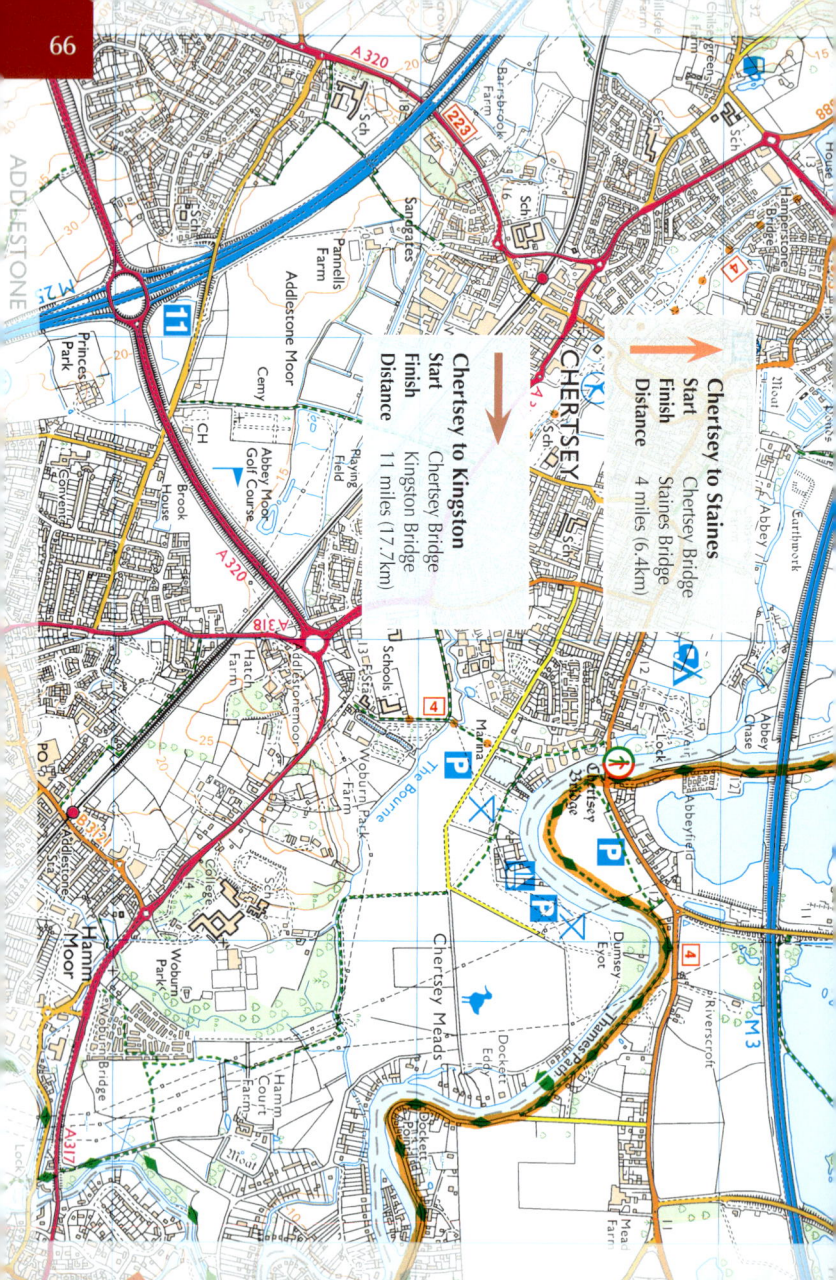

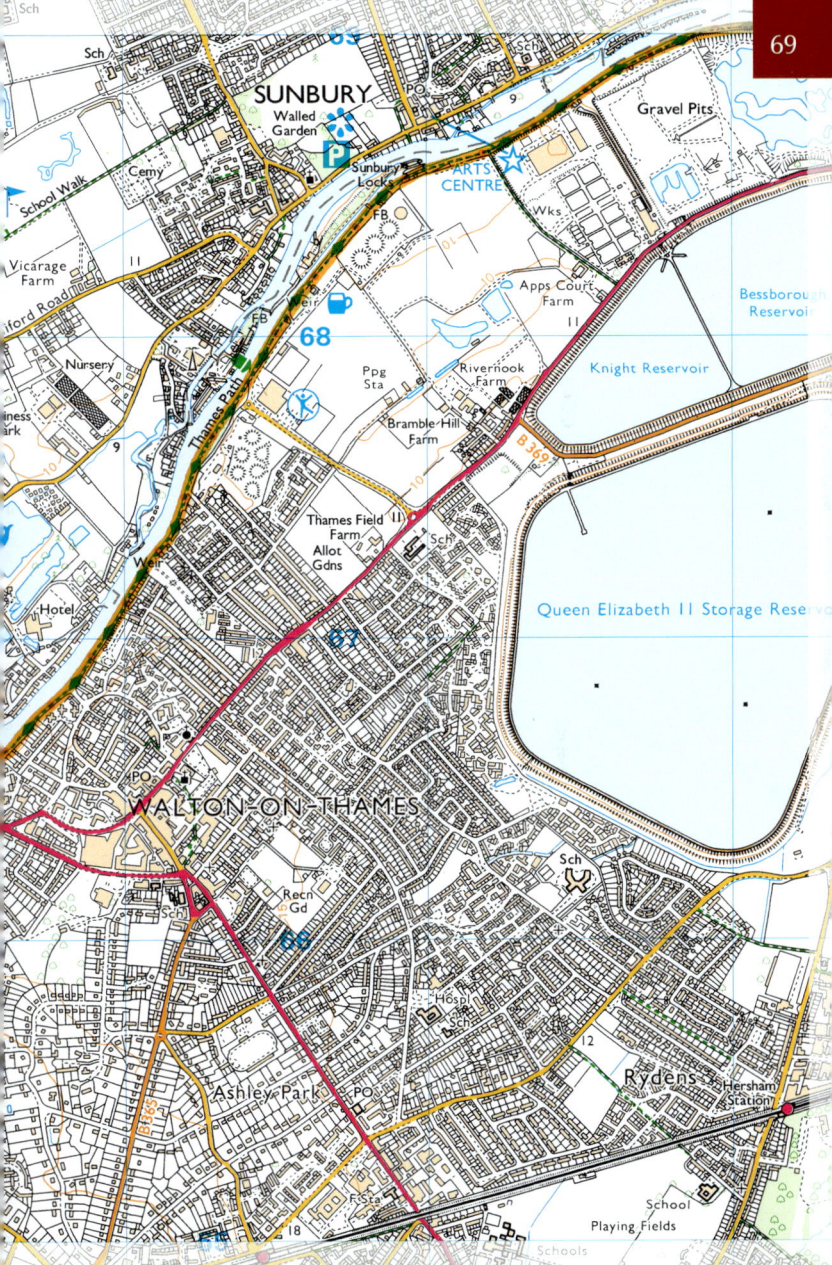

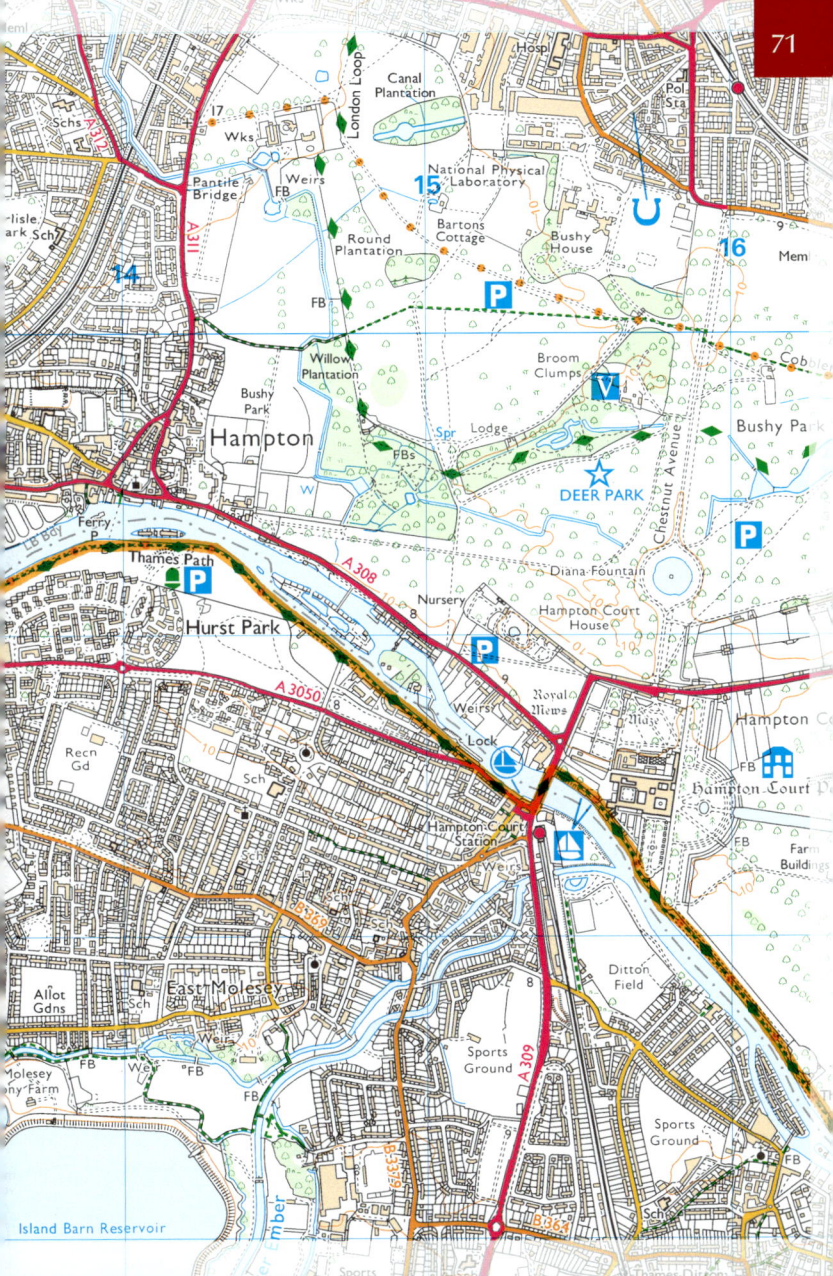

Kingston to Putney
Start Kingston Bridge
Finish Putney Bridge
Distance 13 miles (20.9km)

Kingston to Chertsey
Start Kingston Bridge
Finish Chertsey Bridge
Distance 11 miles (17.7km)

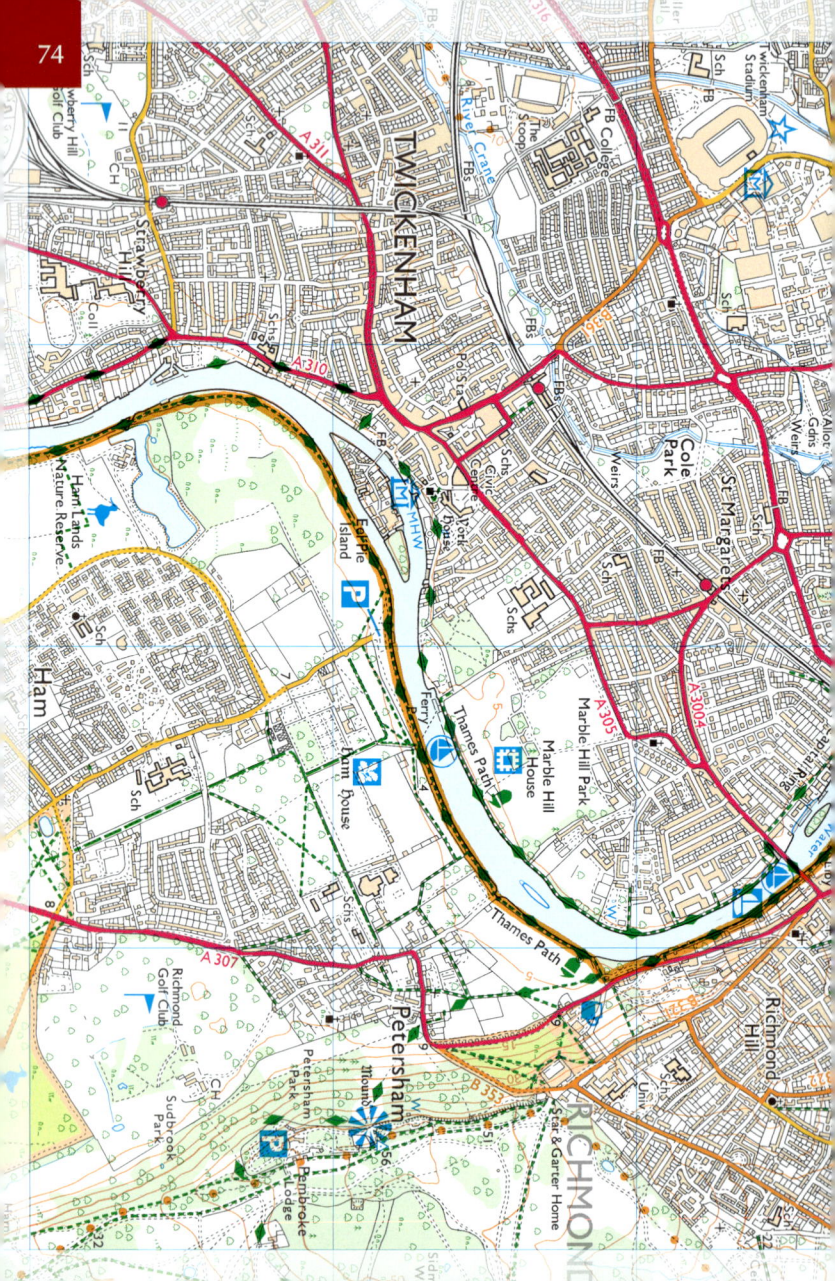

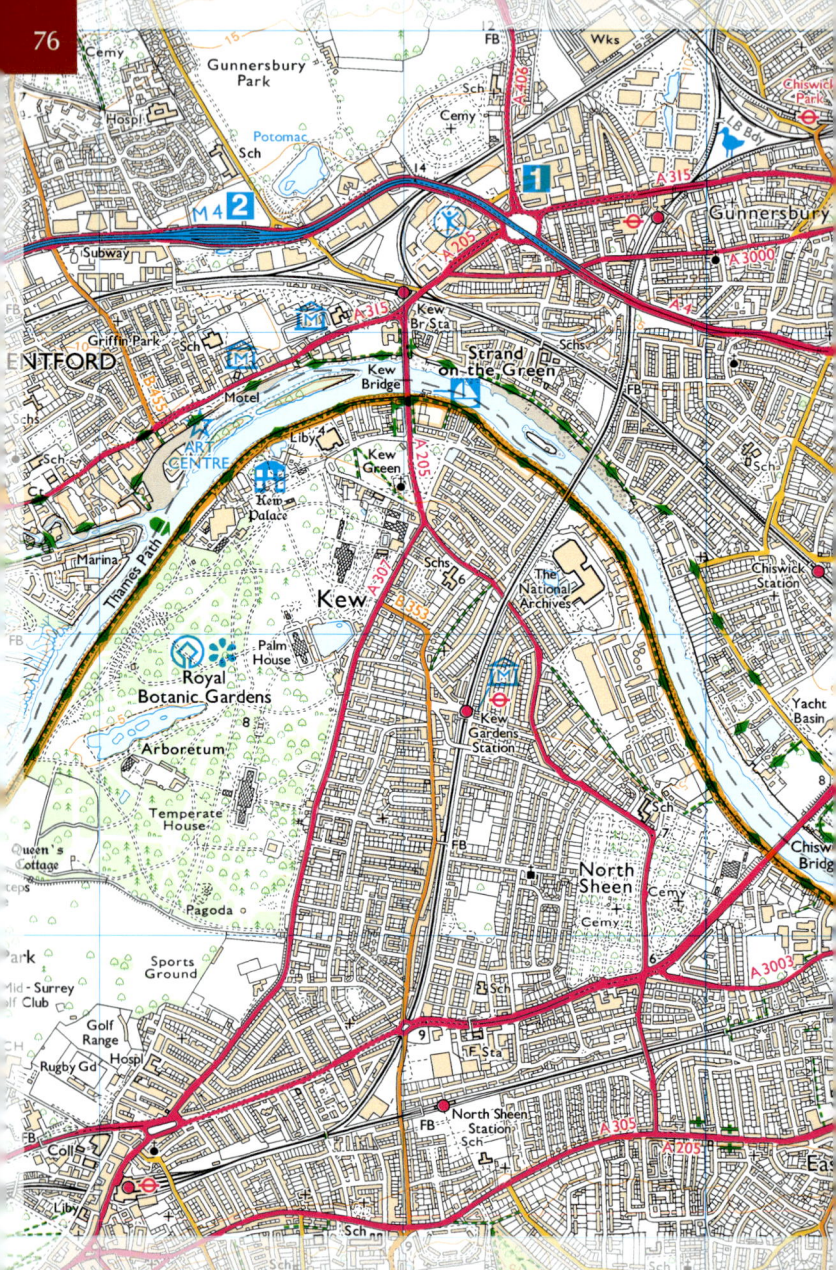

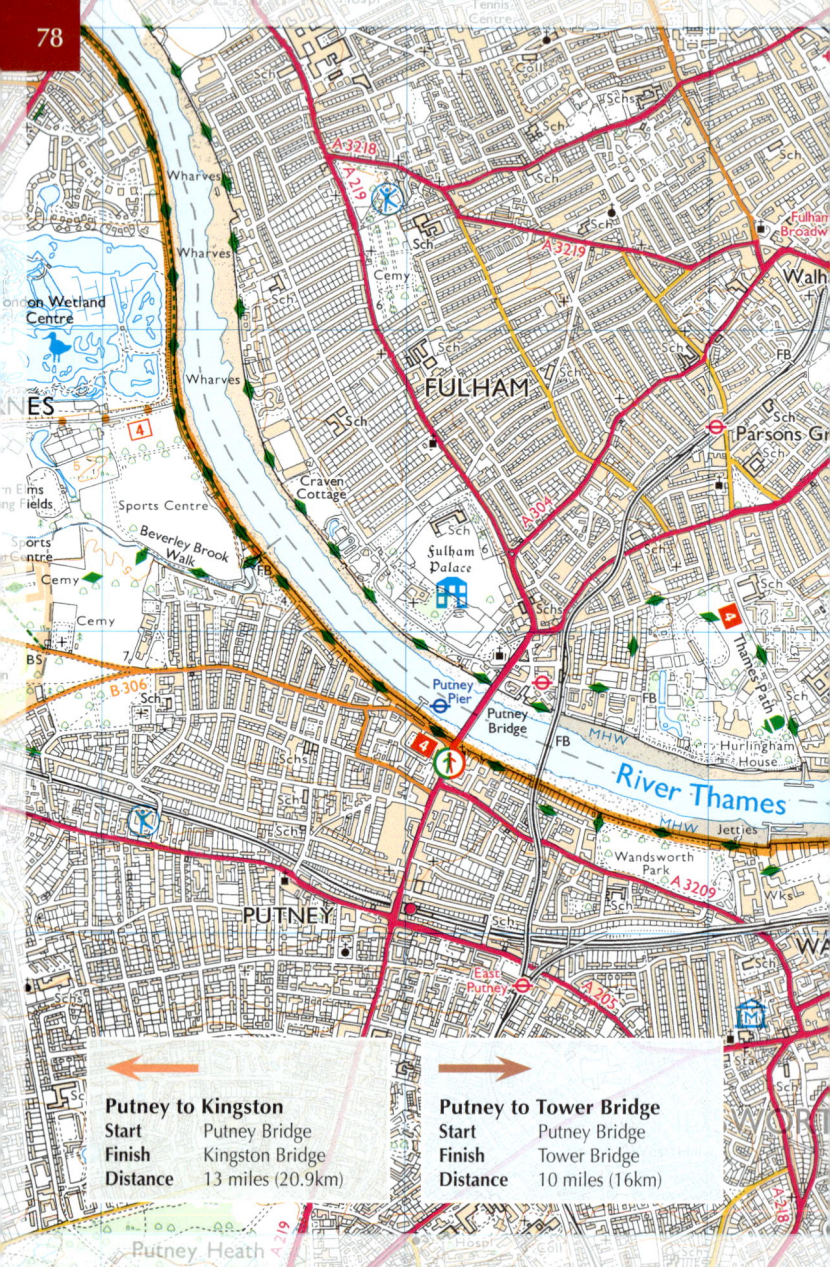

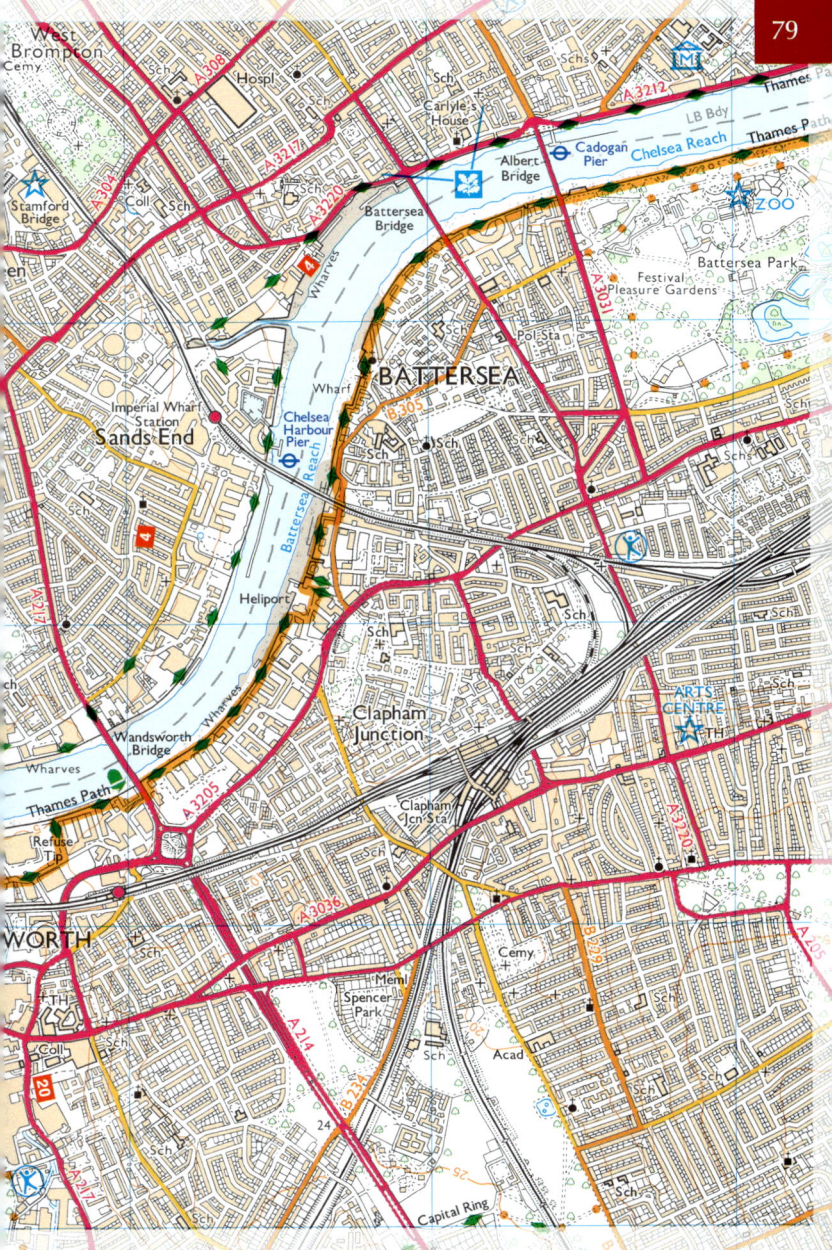

80

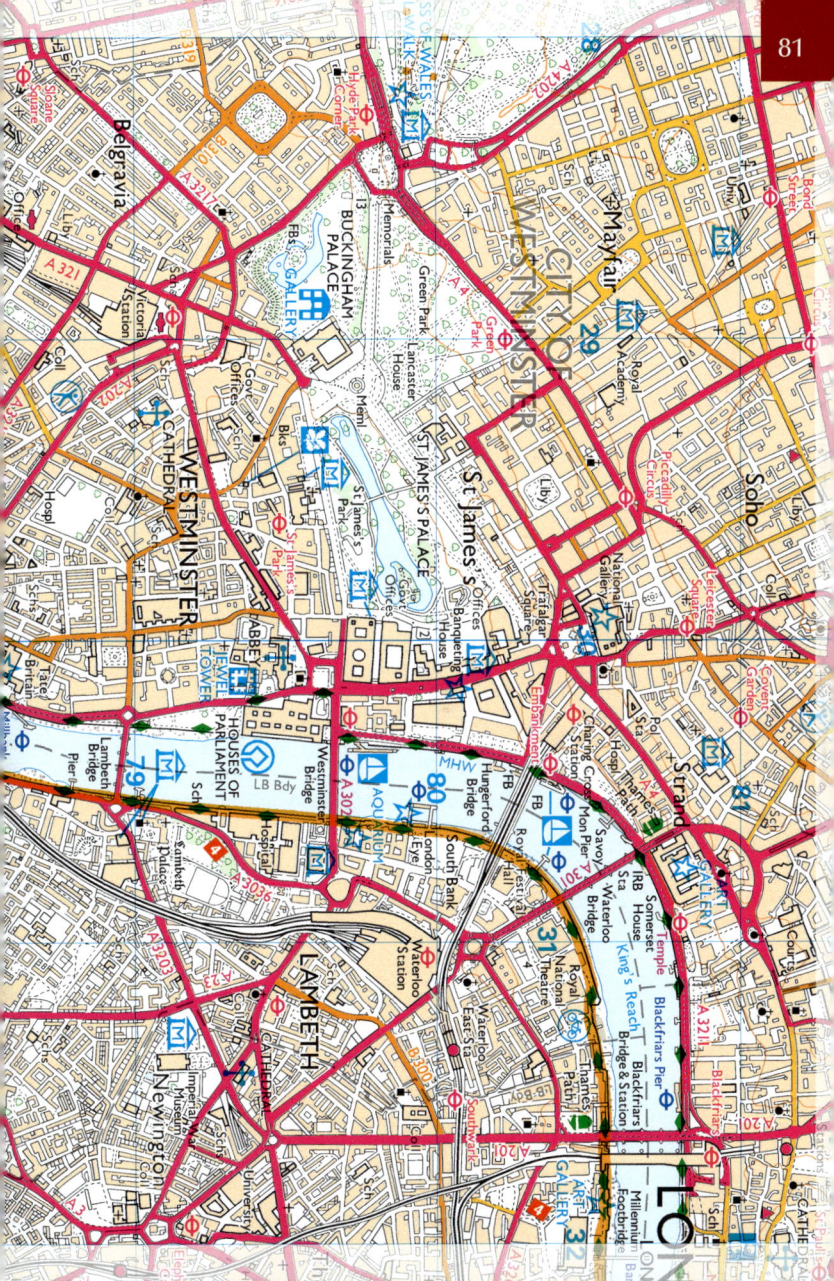

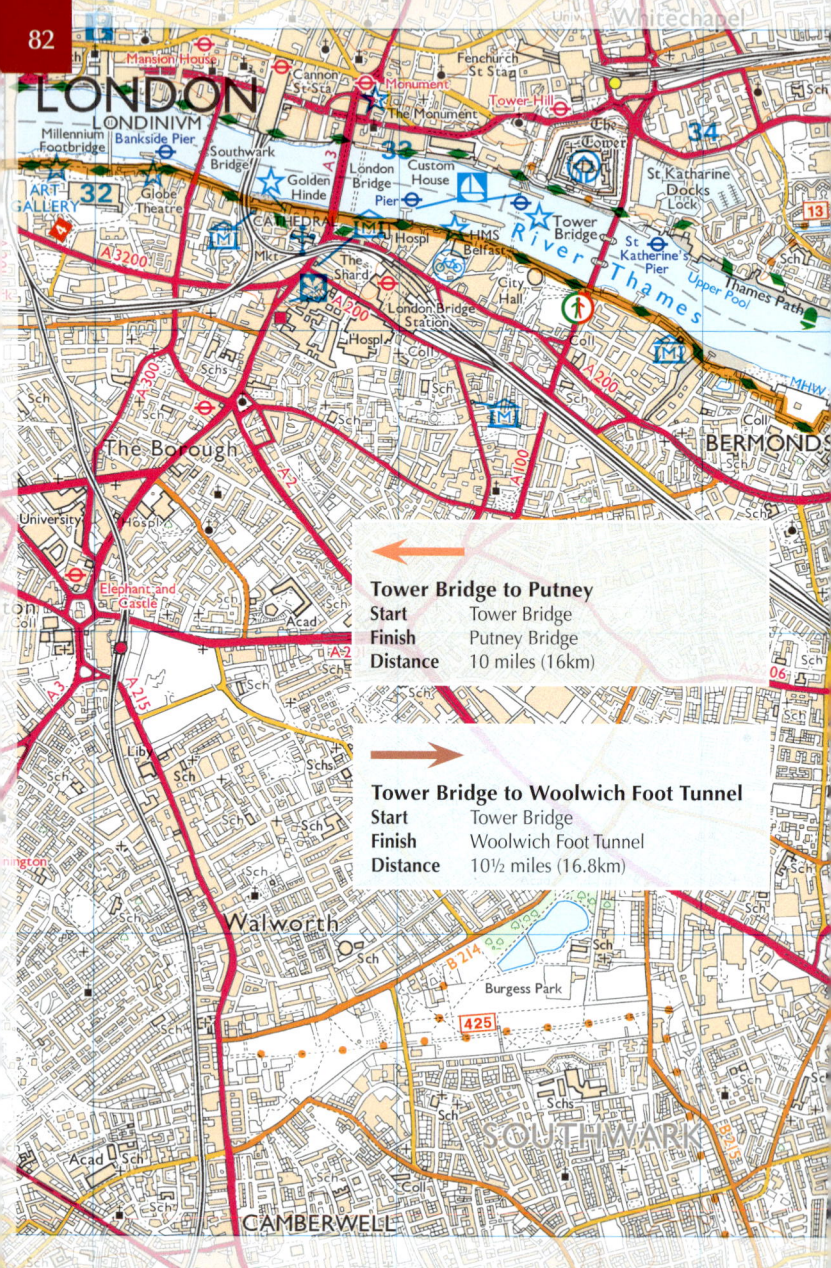

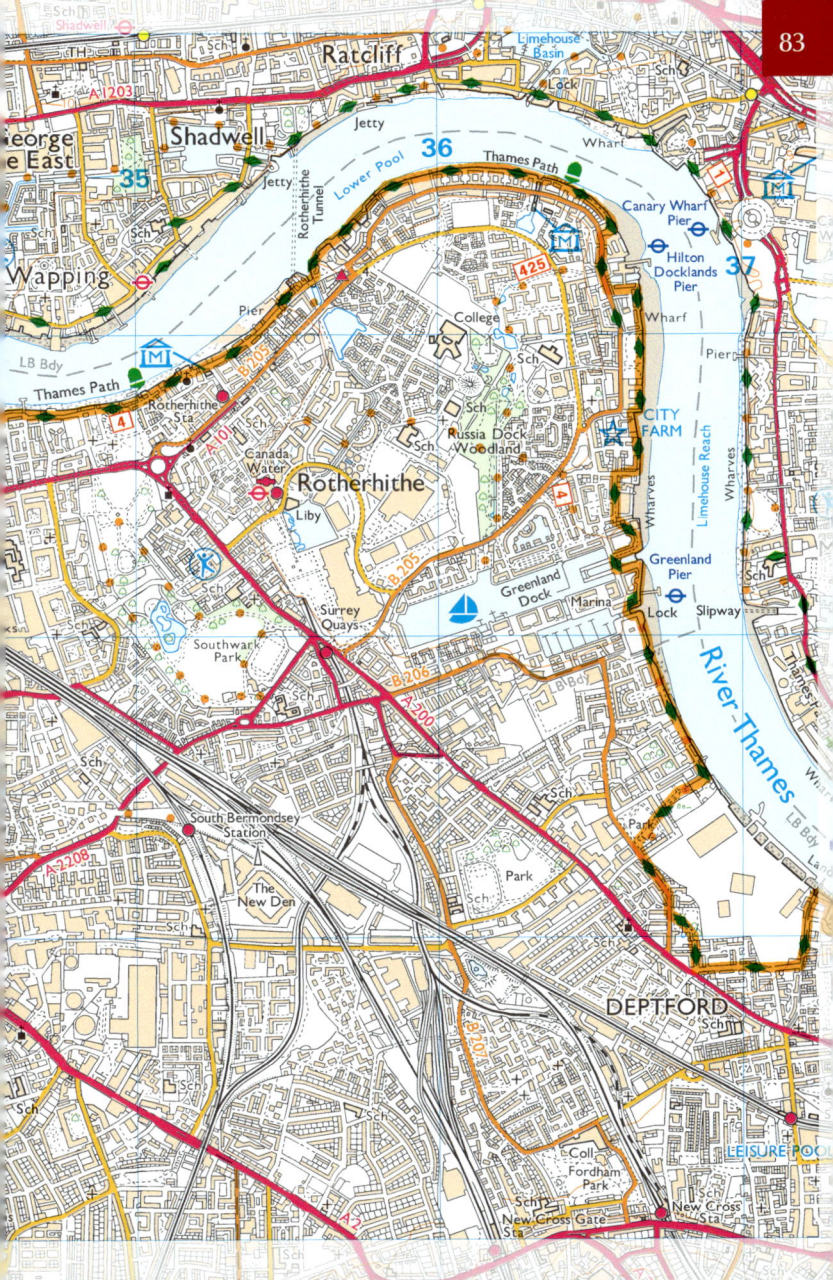

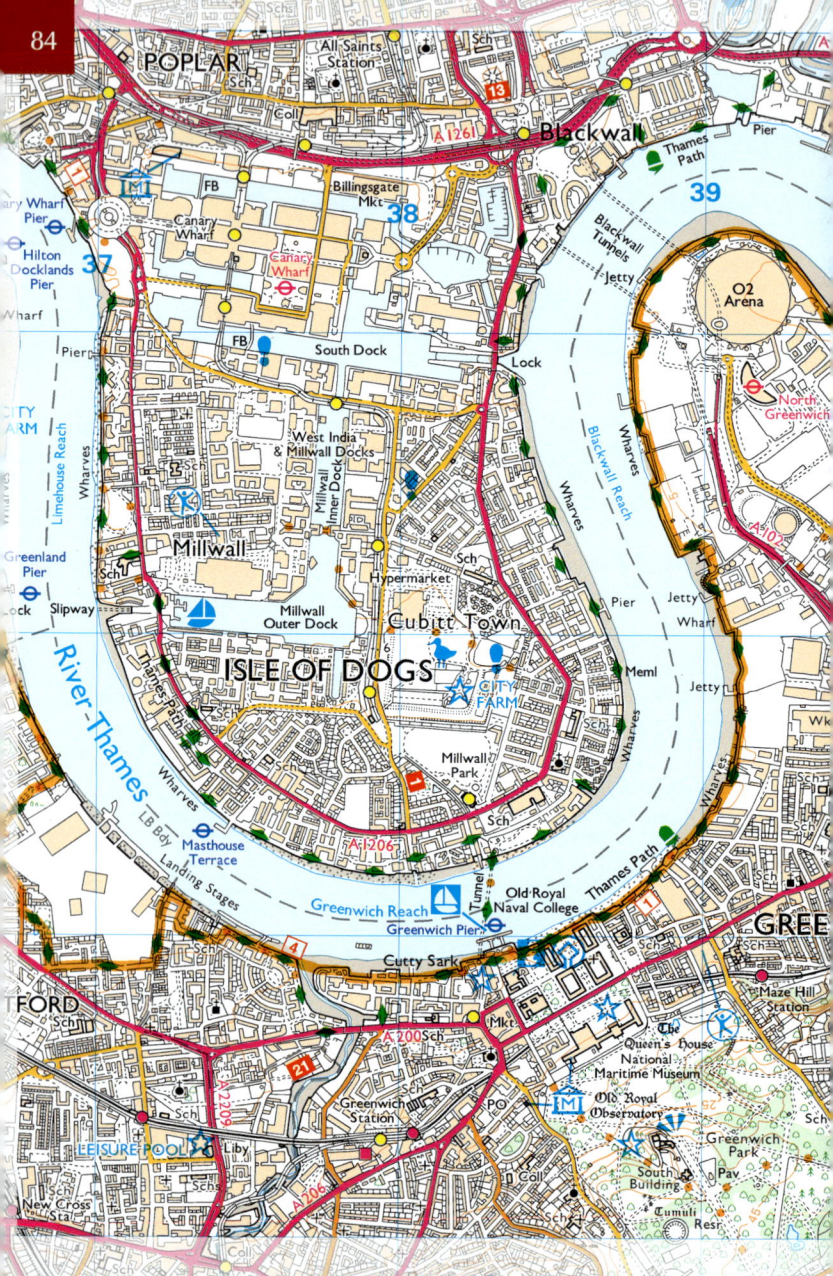

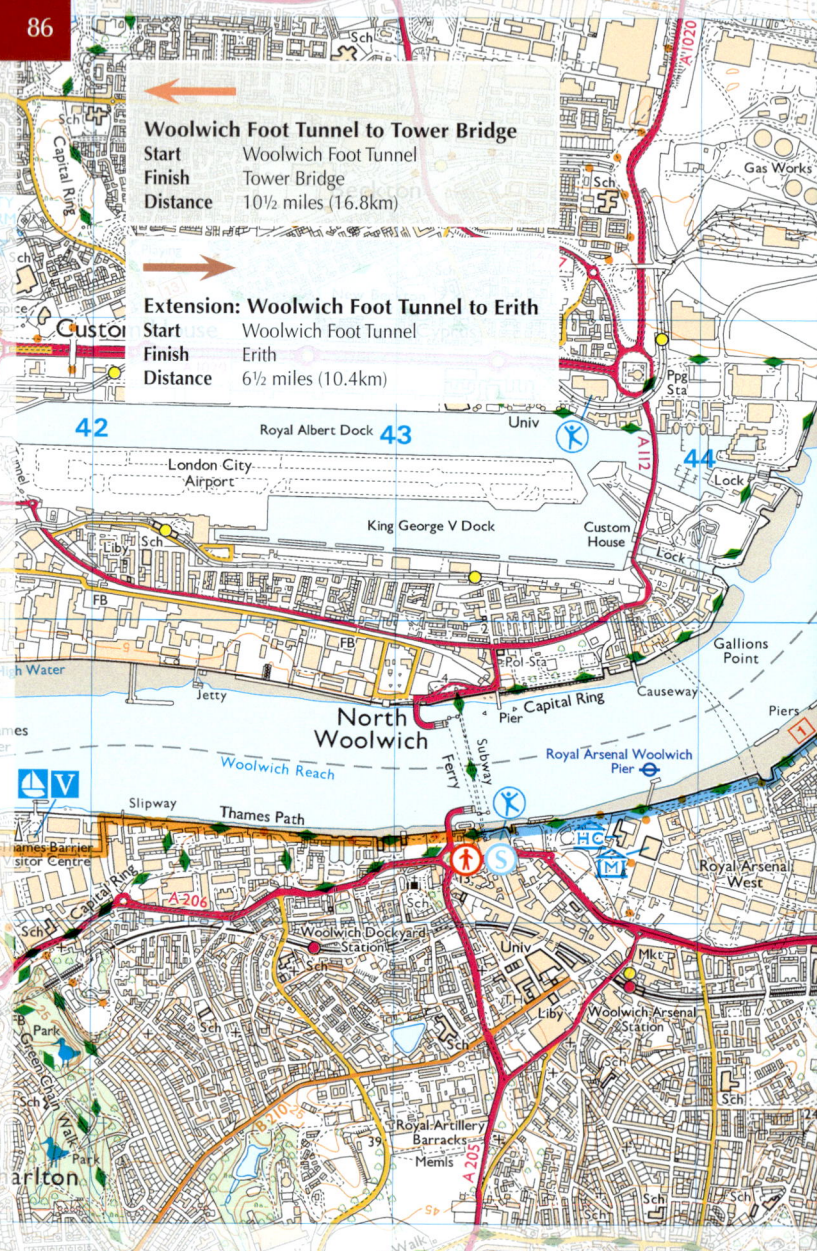

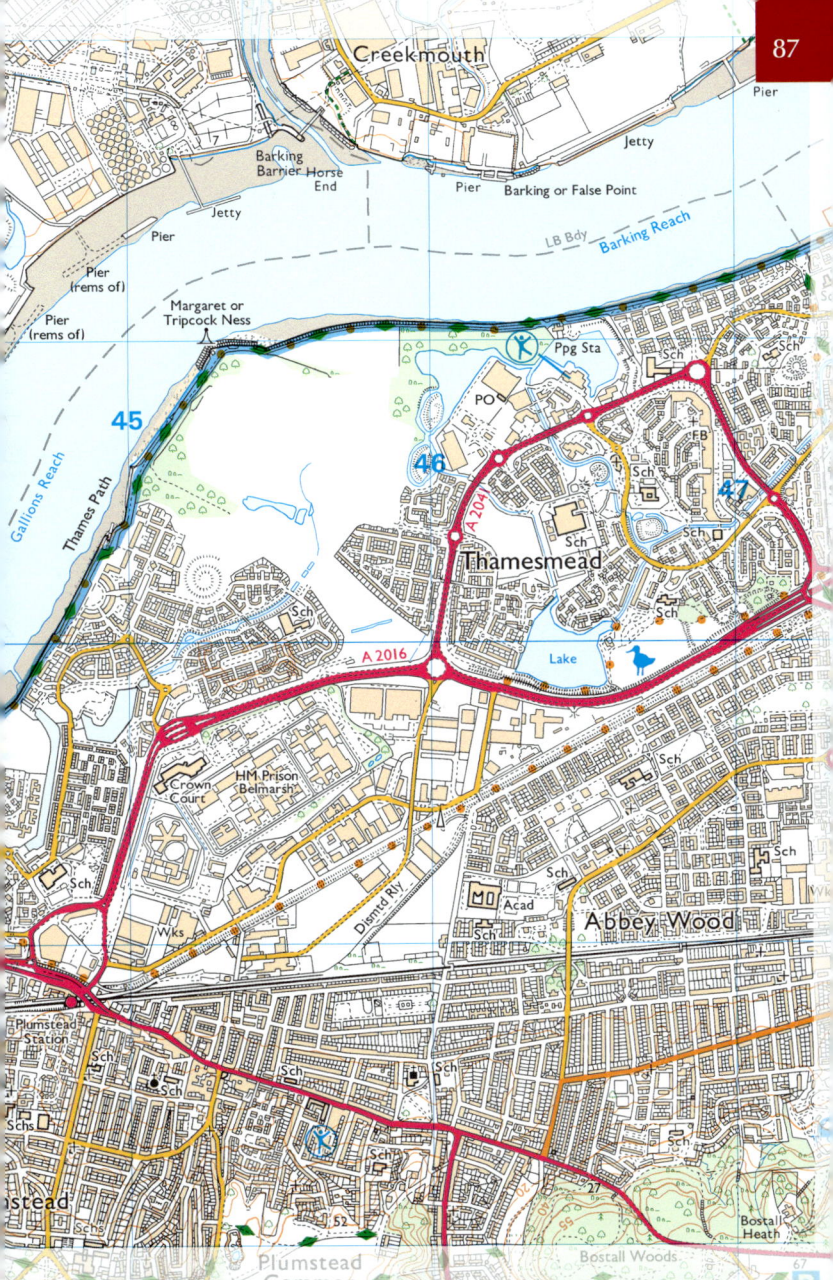

LEGEND OF SYMBOLS USED ON ORDNANCE SURVEY 1:25,000 (EXPLORER) MAPPING

ROADS AND PATHS — Not necessarily rights of way

M1 or A6(M)	Motorway
A 35	Dual carriageway
A30	Main road
B 3074	Secondary road
	Narrow road with passing places
	Road under construction
	Road generally more than 4 m wide
	Road generally less than 4 m wide
	Other road, drive or track, fenced and unfenced
	Gradient: steeper than 20% (1 in 5); 14% (1 in 7) to 20% (1 in 5)
Ferry	Ferry; Ferry P – passenger only
	Path

- **S** Service Area (Motorway)
- **S** Service Area (Main road)
- **7** Junction Number
- **T1** Toll road junction

RAILWAYS

- Multiple track / Single track — standard gauge
- Narrow gauge or Light rapid transit system (LRTS) and station
- Road over; road under; level crossing
- Cutting; tunnel; embankment
- Station, open to passengers; siding

PUBLIC RIGHTS OF WAY

- ─ ─ ─ ─ Footpath
- ─ ─ ─ ─ Bridleway
- +++++ Byway open to all traffic
- ─+─+─ Restricted byway

The representation on this map of any other road, track or path is no evidence of the existence of a right of way

ARCHAEOLOGICAL AND HISTORICAL INFORMATION

Symbol	Description	Symbol	Description	Symbol	Description
⚔	Site of antiquity	VILLA	Roman	☆ ▨	Visible earthwork
⚔ 1066	Site of battle (with date)	𝕮𝖆𝖘𝖙𝖑𝖊	Non-Roman		

Information provided by English Heritage for England and the Royal Commissions on the Ancient and Historical Monuments for Scotland and Wales

OTHER PUBLIC ACCESS

• • •	Other routes with public access	The exact nature of the rights on these routes and the existence of any restrictions may be checked with the local highway authority. Alignments are based on the best information available
♦ ♦ ♦	Recreational route	
♦ ♦ ♦ 🚶 National Trail	(👣) Long Distance Route	
- - - - - - -	Permissive footpath	Footpaths and bridleways along which landowners have permitted public use but which are not rights of way. The agreement may be withdrawn
— — — —	Permissive bridleway	
• • •	Traffic-free cycle route	
1 **1**	National cycle network route number – traffic free; on road	

ACCESS LAND

 Firing and test ranges in the area. Danger! Observe warning notices

 Access permitted within managed controls, for example, local byelaws. Visit www.access.mod.uk for information

England and Wales

 Access land boundary and tint

 Access land in wooded area

 Access information point

Portrayal of access land on this map is intended as a guide to land which is normally available for access on foot, for example access land created under the Countryside and Rights of Way Act 2000, and land managed by the National Trust, Forestry Commission and Woodland Trust. Access for other activities may also exist. Some restrictions will apply; some land will be excluded from open access rights. The depiction of rights of access does not imply or express any warranty as to its accuracy or completeness. Observe local signs and follow the Countryside Code.
Visit www.countrysideaccess.gov.uk for up-to-date information

BOUNDARIES

— + — + —	National
— · — · —	County (England)
— — — —	Unitary Authority (UA), Metropolitan District (Met Dist), London Borough (LB) or District (Scotland & Wales are solely Unitary Authorities)
· · · · · · · ·	Civil Parish (CP) (England) or Community (C) (Wales)
▬▬ ▬▬	National Park boundary

VEGETATION

Limits of vegetation are defined by positioning of symbols

♣ ♣	Coniferous trees
♧ ♧	Non-coniferous trees
ⁿ ⁿ	Coppice
○ ○ ○ ○	Orchard
○ᵣ ○ᵣ	Scrub
⋯⋯	Bracken, heath or rough grassland
⫶⫶	Marsh, reeds or saltings

HEIGHTS AND NATURAL FEATURES

52 ·	Ground survey height	Surface heights are to the nearest metre above mean sea level. Where two heights are shown, the first height is to the base of the triangulation pillar and the second (in brackets) to the highest natural point of the hill
284 ·	Air survey height	

HEIGHTS AND NATURAL FEATURES (continued)

Vertical face/cliff

Loose rock | Boulders | Outcrop | Scree

Contours are at 5 or 10 metre vertical intervals

- Water
- Mud
- Sand; sand and shingle

SELECTED TOURIST AND LEISURE INFORMATION

- Building of historic interest
- Cadw
- Heritage centre
- Camp site
- Caravan site
- Camping and caravan site
- Castle / fort
- Cathedral / Abbey
- Craft centre
- Country park
- Cycle trail
- Mountain bike trail
- Cycle hire
- English Heritage
- Fishing
- Forestry Commission Visitor centre
- Garden / arboretum
- Golf course or links
- Historic Scotland
- Information centre, all year
- Information centre, seasonal
- Horse riding
- Museum
- National Park Visitor Centre (park logo) e.g. Yorkshire Dales
- Nature reserve
- National Trust
- Other tourist feature
- Parking
- Park and ride, all year
- Park and ride, seasonal
- Picnic site
- Preserved railway
- Public Convenience
- Public house/s
- Recreation / leisure / sports centre
- Roman site (Hadrian's Wall only)
- Slipway
- Telephone, emergency
- Telephone, public
- Telephone, roadside assistance
- Theme / pleasure park
- Viewpoint
- Visitor centre
- Walks / trails
- World Heritage site / area
- Water activites
- Boat trips
- Boat hire

(For complete legend and symbols, see any OS Explorer map).

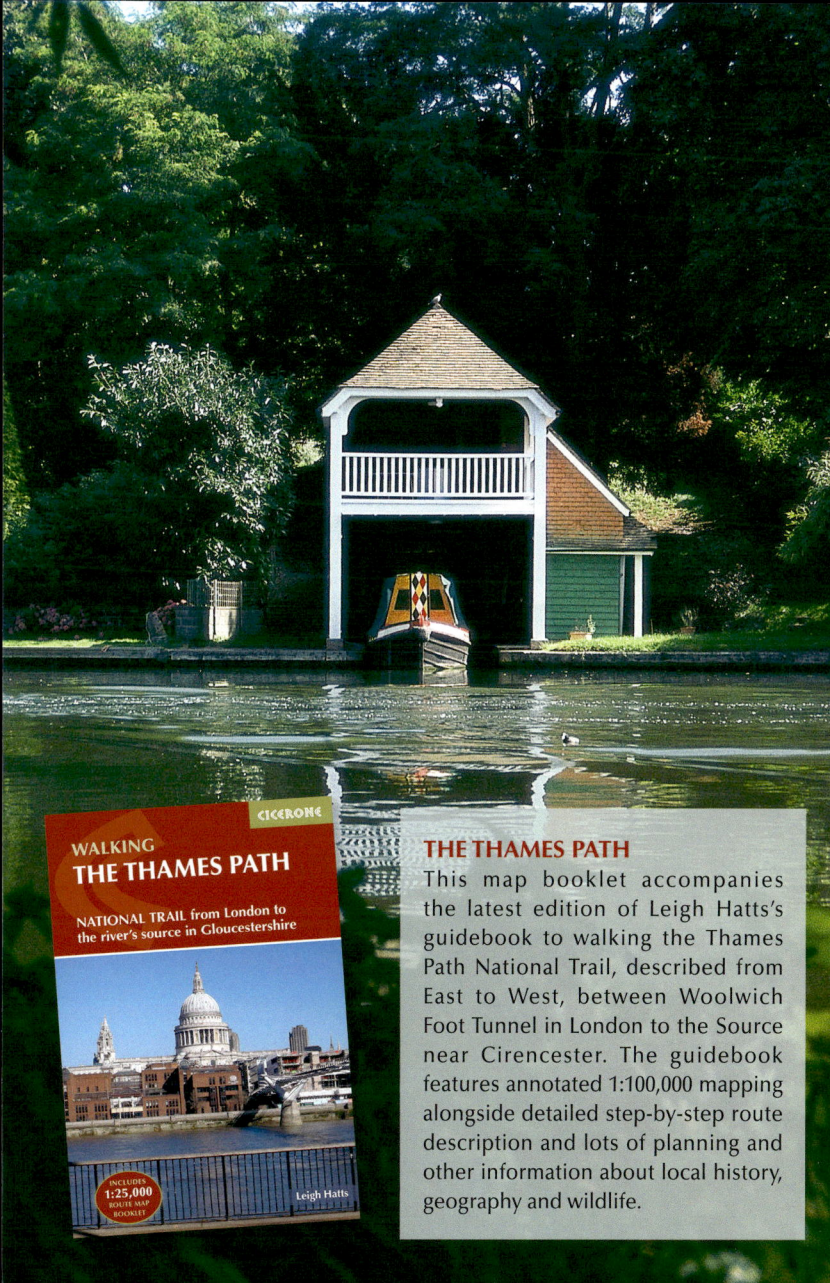

THE THAMES PATH

This map booklet accompanies the latest edition of Leigh Hatts's guidebook to walking the Thames Path National Trail, described from East to West, between Woolwich Foot Tunnel in London to the Source near Cirencester. The guidebook features annotated 1:100,000 mapping alongside detailed step-by-step route description and lots of planning and other information about local history, geography and wildlife.

NOTES

NOTES

OTHER CICERONE TRAIL GUIDES

 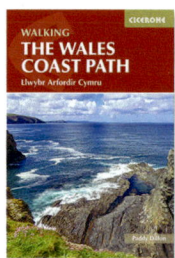 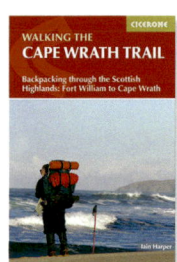

Cicerone National Trails Guides
The South West Coast Path
The South Downs Way
The North Downs Way
The Ridgeway National Trail
The Thames Path
The Cotswold Way
The Peddars Way and
  Norfolk Coast Path
The Cleveland Way and
  the Yorkshire Wolds Way
Cycling the Pennine Bridleway
The Pennine Way
Hadrian's Wall Path
The Pembrokeshire Coast Path
Offa's Dyke Path
Glyndŵr's Way
The Southern Upland Way
The Speyside Way
The West Highland Way
The Great Glen Way

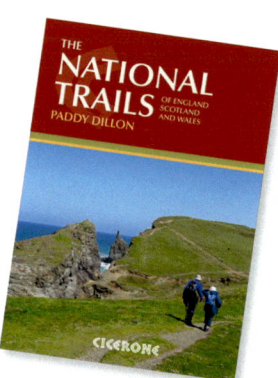

Visit our website for a full
list of Cicerone Trail Guides
www.cicerone.co.uk